MODERN HANDBOOK OF LIBRARY & INFORMATION SCIENCE

MODERN HANDBOOK OF LIBRARY & INFORMATION SCIENCE

Poonam

AKANSHA PUBLISHING HOUSE
NEW DELHI • GUWAHATI • VISAKHAPATNAM

AKANSHA PUBLISHING HOUSE
4649-B/21, Ansari Road
Darya Ganj, New Delhi - 110 002
Ph.: 23263193 / 9811582579 / 09435116718
Fax: 011-23263193
Email: ektabooks@yahoo.com
www.akanshapublishinghouse.com

Modern Handbook of Library & Information Science

First Published 2010
ISBN 978-81-8370-233-1

PRINTED IN INDIA

Published by Akansha Publishing House, New Delhi and Printed at Harmain Offset Press

To
S.R. Ranganathan
The Father of Library Science
in India & a Universal Librarian
This book is Humbly dedicated

Contents

PREFACE

> "We sow our thoughts and reap our actions. We sow our actions and reap our habits. We sow our habits and reap our characters. We sow our characters and reap our destiny."
>
> —C.A. Hall

Libraries are the repository of knowledge. Though with the advent of automation and use of latest communication technologies, the functions of modern libraries has gone drastic change. For a library practitioner it is necessary to know the functions of libraries of yore days as well as modern developments.

In fact, a library shares many items of administrative routine with other offices, for example, those relating to personnel, finance, accounts, correspondence, printing, stationery, supplies and services, and building and equipment. A library is usually a dependent body. Therefore, the routine about most of these items may have to be in conformity with that of the parent-body. In the case of a public library, the Local Body is likely to be the Local Library Authority. It prescribes the routine.

For efficient functioning, the work behind the screen should be done systematically and expeditiously. For, the maximum possible time should be saved to attend to readers, in conformity with the Fourth Law of Library Science. Further, every item of routine should be revised, to avoid errors. Otherwise, the cumulation of errors through time will be injurious to the efficiency and the reputation of the library.

Amidst a plethora of literature, the present endeavour is unique which compiles judiciously selected readings on a variety of issues that every library professional must be acquainted with.

The main topics covered under this are—Traditional Functions of Libraries; Documentation of International Comparative Statistics; Procurement Process; Guidelines for Software and System Selection; Professionalism in Service Providing; Information Technology and Library Documentation; New Technology for Library and Information Science; Miscellaneous Issues; Intellectual Property and Copyrights; Appendix; and Bibliography etc. Thus, it has become a perfect handbook.

We hope this will serve a dependable tool of reference to all students, teachers and professionals in the field of library and information science.

With the sole aim of furnishing authentic information we have consulted a number of standard works on the theme, penned by the great men of letters. By sharing their views and findings all the users of the book will be benefitted immensely.

We express our gratitude to all those whose works are cited or substantially made use of in the present work. We are equally grateful to librarians and other officials of different libraries for making available the requisite information. I am grateful to my teachers and friends for their inspiration, guidance and help. I express my gratitude to my publisher for undertaking publication of this venture and materialising it into present form.

—Poonam

1

TRADITIONAL FUNCTIONS OF LIBRARIES

> "The power of words is immense. A well-chosen word has often sufficed to stop a flying army, to change a defeat into victory, and to save an empire."
>
> —**Emile de Girardin**

Libraries are the repository of knowledge. Though with the advent of automation and use of latest communication technologies, the functions of modern libraries has gone drastic change. For a library practioner it is necessary to know the functions of libraries of yore days.

In fact, a library shares many items of administrative routine with other offices, for example, those relating to personnel, finance, accounts, correspondence, printing, stationery, supplies and services, and building and equipment. A library is usually a dependent body. Therefore, the routine about most of these items may have to be in conformity with that of the parent-body. In the case of a public library, the Local Body is likely to be the Local Library Authority. It prescribes the routine.

The work behind the screen should be done systematically and expeditiously. For, the maximum possible time should be saved to attend to readers, in conformity with the Fourth Law of Library Science. Further, every item of routine should be revised, to avoid errors. Otherwise, the cumulation of errors through time will be injurious to the efficiency and the reputation of the library.

Branch Library

A branch library should have only the following items of work behind the screen:

1. The receipt of the current issues of periodical publications;
2. Maintenance of the stack-room.
3. Maintenance of the building and the stores.

All other work behind the screen should be done by the central library. As a result, the staff of a branch library should be able to devote practically all its time to circulation work, reference service, and extension work. This will satisfy the Fourth Law.

Central Library

Even a city or district central library should spend only minimum time in classification and cataloguing. This will be made possible by the system of centralised classification and cataloguing coming into vogue in the country. Thus the books will arrive at the city and district central libraries with the call numbers printed in the back of the title-page and tooled on the spine. Printed catalogue cards for all the book entries will also come along from the State Central Library. At any rate, they can be bought from that Library.

BOOK-SELECTION

Remarkably, the first step in the distinctive part of library administration relates to book-selection. This is conditioned by three factors:

1. The demand, in the light of local interest, in different areas of the field of knowledge.
2. The supply or the extent and nature of the availability of books in the market, preference always being given to sumptuous editions on good paper with large type and plenty of illustrations; and
3. The total finance available and the proportion in which it is allocated to different subjects and standards in relation to the strength or weakness of the already existing collection in the various subjects and standards.

Ascertaining Demand

The subject-distribution of the circulation of books in the library will give a picture of the demand current in the locality. The library should also anticipate potential demand by studying the happenings in the locality, in the country and in the world, and the special festivals and celebrations expected to occur in the year. The amount for books should be allocated for different subjects in the light of the details arrived at in assessing the demand. Without making undue deviation from the prevailing reading standard and taste, the library should seek to elevate them progressively, in small *quanta* by its book-selection standards.

Sources

The chief sources for selection of books in English are the *Bookseller and* the *Publisher's circular* of Great Britain and the *Publisher's weekly* of the United States, which are weeklies; also the *English catalogue* of Great Britain and the *Wilson's catalogue* of the. United States, which are available as annuals. The chief sources for selection of books published in India are the *Quarterly* list of publications issued by the Registrars of Books of the Constituent States and the Indian National Bibliography and the State Bibliography of each State publishing it. Other sources of both kinds of books are the catalogues of individual publishers and booksellers; the bibliographies in books; independent bibliographies; and book reviews in periodicals. The Sunday editions of the *Dailies* in India contain literary pages in which reviews are published.

Suggestion Tray

Books of probable interest to the readers are likely to be brought to the notice of the library by the readers themselves. When the suggestion reaches the library, a book selection card should be prepared and filed in the suggestion-tray in a classified sequence.

Routine

The sources for book selection should be scanned systematically as and when they become available and a book-selection card should be prepared for each selected item. It should be roughly classified and its standard symbol (like elementary, ordinary, advanced, and so on) should also be tentatively put on the card. These cards should be filed in a classified sequence in different sets according to the standard. The accumulated cards should be discussed at convenient intervals — say once in a month on the appointed day—with the concerned specialists and the sanction of the Library Committee or the Librarian, as the case may be, should be obtained for the finally prepared Indent.

Weeding Out

The printed sources should be systematically filed on shelves. As and when a new edition of the source arrives, the old edition should be discarded in the case of ephemeral materials or removed to the bibliographical collection if they are worth the retention.

Forms and Registers

Look Selection Card. Printed, 6 pt type. Bristol Board, white for purchased books, green for gift books. Red for bound volumes of periodicals. The text on one side should be as shown below:

The text on the other side be as follows:

Ac N Don N Wl N

Cl N

Auth

Title

Size Coll Ed Yr

Pub Pub price

Series etc

Review

Reference

Vendor Cost

Date Inits Indian

Order N Foreign

Sel Voucher N

Apprd

Order

Recd

Paid

Accnd

Cut

Clasd

Cat

Shld

Bound

Wl

Book selection consultation letter form. Stencil. 21 lb. Printing paper. White. The text of the form is as follows:

Subject: Book Selection

I have the honour to enclose herewith (number) book selection cards in (subject) for your consideration. Please be good enough to sort them into

The three group "approved" "daferred", and "rejected". The three group may be separately bundled and sent to me along with a covering letter embodying your recommendation.

The balance available for purchase of books in your subject within the current financial year is Rs....

Expecting your reply within a week.

Indent noting form. Stencil. 21 lb. Printing paper. White. The text of the form is as follows:

Outside N	Dated ....
File N	Date of receipt....

Subject: Indent for books

Librarian's note	*Office note*
N of items recommended	
N of items already available or on order	
N of items recommended for duplication	
Estimated cost of the items not in library	Rs
Estimated cost of the duplications recommended	Rs
Total estimated cost	Rs
Allotment for books	Rs
Amount already appropriated	Rs
Balance available	Rs
Remarks	

Library Committee's decision

Note: If the librarian is the sanctioning authority, the last line may be omitted. In the first column, the words and "Sanction" may be added after "Note".

Daily diary. Its headings should be the following:

1. Letters received
2. Letters replied
3. Letters filed
4. Letters drafted
5. Routine letters issued
6. Reminders sent
7. Indents called for
8. Indents received
9. Book selection cards checked with selected cards tray
10. Book selection cards checked with order tray
11. Books selection cards checked with bills on hand
12. Book selection cards checked with catalogue

S16 *Weekly diary.* This should show the number of books selection cards written. Its headings must be the symbols for the main classes of classification used.

Files

Name	*Amplifying device*	*Filing characteristic*
Sources	Subject Device or/ and Language Device	Correspondent
Selion	Subject Device	
Indent	Do	Do
Allotment	Do	Do

Outward enquiries	Do	Do
Inward enquiries	Do	Do

All these files may be transferred to the record sequence one year after it is closed. They may be destroyed after three or five years according to convenience.

BOOK-ORDER

The work of ordering books in Indian libraries is at present more difficult than it is elsewhere. It is English and American books that figure most in them. Thus, the chief book-markets are thousands of miles away in far-off London and New York. As a result, Indian Libraries are not able to get books on approval or to choose between different editions by actual inspection of books. The task of deciding whether a new edition is substantially different from the one already in the library becomes extremely difficult. The Book-Order Section in Indian libraries has therefore to take a much greater responsibility and put in much more work in checking the indents with the stock, than in European and American libraries. Of late however, a few enterprising booksellers have begun to stock general books in important state capitals, such as Bombay, Calcutta, Delhi, Lucknow and Madras.

In the matter of Indian publications, the situation is even worse. The publishing trade is not yet properly organised in India except for text-books. In many cases, the author himself has to play the role of publisher and bookseller. He may live in an out-of-the-way place, and as may be expected, he has not developed business methods. Not infrequently it happens that he does not respond at all to orders.

Standing Vendors

It is a moot point whether it is advantageous for a library to buy its books directly from the publishers or through a standing vendor. In the case of most books, there may be an advantage to have a standing vendor. The Library Authority should select the standing vendor once in three years. The choice should be settled by the competence of the vendor to make complete and prompt supply. There should be a clause in the contract for the cancellation of the contract for delay of more than three months. After the introduction of net-book agreement, the monetary terms of the contract will be simple and uniform. Even till then, the pestering practice of calling for tenders for every order should not be adopted.

Contract

It is necessary to stipulate certain conditions of a bibliographical nature in appointing standing vendors. They should be asked to undertake the following responsibilities:

0. The contract is liable to be cancelled if the supply is not completed within three months of the order;
1. Every volume should be carefully collated before being sent. If any defect is discovered at this end, they should take back the defective copy and supply a sound copy at their own cost, including the to and fro freight;
2. The latest edition of the book is to be supplied, unless there are specific instructions to the contrary;
3. If the order contains a note that a certain edition of a particular book is already in the library, they should find out if the later edition in the market is substantially different from the one in the library. If not, the book should not be supplied, but an advice should be sent. In cases of doubt, they should state the case and supply the book only after receiving a confirmatory order;

4. If the book is a reissue of another book under a different title, they should advise the library about it and send the supply only after receiving a confirmatory order;
5. If a book is an off-print from a periodical publication or another book, they should advise the library about it and send the supply only after receiving a confirmatory order;
6. If a book is really a foreign publication, though listed in the trade lists of their country by the local representatives of the foreign publisher, they should advise the library about it and send the supply only after receiving a confirmatory order;
7. If there is any difference in the name or in the spelling of the name of the author or in the title, they should advise the library about it and send the supply only after receiving a confirmatory order;
8. If any book occurs in more than one order or is covered by any of the standing orders, only one copy should be sent and a second copy should not be sent without getting a confirmatory order; and
9. In all these cases, if they send a wrong supply, they should take it back at their own cost.

Second-hand Books

In the matter of out-of-print books, it is best to obtain quotations from different second-hand booksellers and decide the vendor in each case on its merits, rather than appoint a single standing vendor. Very often the catalogues of the second-hand booksellers may obviate even the necessity for enquiry. But these catalogues should not be relied upon, if the amount is considerable. It may be possible to get better terms by obtaining competitive quotations.

Ordering

It is desirable that order-work is distributed evenly throughout the year and an order is sent out regularly once in a week or a month on an appointed day. The routine for each order may be as follows: Arrange the finally sanctioned book-selection cards alphabetically by the names of authors and check carefully to eliminate unintended duplications of all kinds. For this purpose, check with the

1. Catalogue of the library;
2. Standing-order-cards;
3. Outstanding-order-cards;
4. Bills awaiting payment; and
5. Exchange list of the library if any.

Separate the cards for the books which can be got as gifts and apply for them. Type four copies of the order-list for the surviving cards, send one with the order to the vendor. Leave one for use in advising readers. Use the third as office copy. File the fourth copy behind a guide showing the week in which the supply is due. This will be used for the Vigilance Work described in section Vigilence Work.

The corresponding book-selection cards now gain the status of order cards. Insert these in their proper alphabetical places, in the order tray which contains the outstanding cards.

Standing Order

It is desirable to give standing orders for the following classes of books:

1. *Series-books,* i.e. belonging to a series all the volumes of which the library has decided to buy;
2. *Multi-volumed books,* i.e. books in two or more volumes

all the volumes of which are not published simultaneously;

3. *Instalment-books,* ie books published in successive parts or fascicules which should be accumulated in the library and bound after the title-page arrives;
4. *Subscription-books,* i.e. books for which advance payment is to be made either in full or in part before actual publication.

Receiving the Supply

When the supply arrives, arrange the books in the sequence in which they are entered in the bill. Lift the order card of each book from the order tray and insert it on its title-page. If there is no order card for a book, it has been either already paid for or it was never ordered. When all the books have got their respective cards, carefully collate the books, scrutinise and approve them only if they answer to every detail furnished in the respective order cards. Then pass the books on for classification, cataloguing, and shelf-registering. Defects may also be detected at this stage. Hence, defer cutting, stamping, accessioning and payment till those processes are over. Retain the order cards with you. They form the control to ensure that all the books come back for accessioning. Various difficulties may crop up in this work.

Supply of Standing Order

The procedure for receiving supplies of standing order, and watching their regular supply, should be similar to the one described in section "Periodical Publications".

Vigilance Work

As soon as a book order is sent out, file the fourth copy of the order in the Book-Order Vigilance Pad behind the week-guide of the due date of supply. The files behind a week-guide are to be arranged on the basis of the following successive characteristics: (1) Vendor; (2) Order number; and (3) Order Date. The due date also should be filled up at that time. The items received should be ticked as and when the supply or report arrives. It may not arrive all at one time. In every week in which some items lie un-ticked, shift the vigilance order copy to the proper place behind the next week-guide. After the supply is completed it may be destroyed.

Forms and Registers

Standing order card. Manuscript. Bristol board. White. Tray. Front side 7 lines. Back side" 18 lines.

Row headings at the top of the front side:

First line: Series Heading

Second line: SO N ...... dated ..... Period

Third line: Vendor .... Note

Column headings for the remaining part of the first side and for the back side:

Serial Vol N (12 cm). Accession N (18 cm). Voucher N and Date (25 cm). Call N (30 cm). Heading (30 cm). Price (6 cm).

Order form to standing vendors. Stencil. 21 lb. Printing paper. White. The text of the form is as follows:

Subject: Book Order

Please supply the... Library under the usual conditions with the books in the enclosed lists, viz

Order Number Dated Remarks

S25 *Weekly diary (Routine).* Its headings should be the following:

1. Letters received
2. Letters replied
3. Letters filed
4. Letters drafted
5. Routine letters issued
6. Reminders sent
7. Indents received
8. Indents returned
9. Book order cards checked with outstanding order tray
10. Book order cardschecked with standing order cards
11. Book order cards checked with bills on hand
12. Book order cards checked with exchange list
13. Book order cards checked with catalogue
14. Book order cards checked with shelf
12. Standing orders issued for series books
16. Standing orders issued for muitivolumed books
17. Standing orders issued for instalment books
18. Standing orders issued for subscription books
19. Order cards filed
20. Ordinary books received from vendor
21. Series books received from vendor
22. Muitivolumed books received from vendor 6664
23. Fascicules of instalment of books received from vendor
24. Subscription books received from vendor
25. Volumes and cards transmitted to the accession section
26. *Weekly diary (Subject).* Its headings must consist of

the symbols for the main divisions of the book classification used or some suitable modification of them.

Files

Name	*Class Number*		*Filing Characteristic*
Standing vendors	21	(Subject Device)	Vendor
Standing vendors (Second hand books)	218	do	do
Enquities and quotations	22	do	Heading
Ordinary books ordering	23	do	Vendor and date of order
Ordinary books order doubt clearing	234	do	Heading
Serious ordering	241	do	Series heading
Muitivolumed books ordering	242	do	Heading
Instalment books ordering	243	do	do
Prepublication ordering	244	do	do
Gift books	28		Donor
Outward enquiries	291		Correspondent
Inward enquiries	292		do

The files may be transferred to the record sequence one year after disposal and destroyed five years thereafter.

PERIODICAL PUBLICATIONS

In fact, Periodicals are prone to develop idiosyncrasies of several kinds. Of these, irregularity in publication and supply affects the administrative routine most. If the non-receipt of a particular issue is not brought to the notice of the publisher promptly, there is a great probability of the library never getting it.

Hence the greatest amount of vigilance and promptness is necessary in dealing with periodical publications, and it must be achieved without undue dependence on mere memory. It is best done by means of a simple Three Card System. A card 125 × 75 mm will last for 6 years for weeklies and for twenty-five years for monthlies, if they are ruled on both sides. It may not be worth-while to bind and preserve all the periodicals. What must be preserved should be decided by the authorities.

Renewal Order

It is desirable not to change the list of current periodicals violently from year to year. A periodical which it has been decided to have bound and preserved should not be light-heartedly discontinued in one year and renewed in another year. Thus most of the periodicals should be given a standing order. It is conducive to good business to send a renewal order once in a year on an appointed day and call for bills for subscription. For subscriptions of most periodicals are payable in advance. This is enforced by the publishers since they cannot otherwise decide how many copies they should print. Foreign periodicals will, therefore, have to be renewed even in October so that payment may reach the other side before the year begins. For convenience of routine it is better to renew Indian periodicals also in October.

Three Card System

The prompt receipt of the current issues of each periodical publication is to be watched with vigilance. Vigilance is best practised by the Three-Card System in a big library and by a Two Card System in a small library. One of these cards is called the Registered Card. Its use is described in section 533. Its structure is given in section 537. The second card is called the Check Card. Its use is described in section 534. Its structure is given in section 537. The third card to be used in a large library is called the Classified Index Card.

Registering

As soon as the mail arrives each day, after satisfying yourself that each packet is addressed to the library, open the wrapper of each and insert it in the periodical. Arrange the periodicals alphabetically by the title. The rest of the work is to be done for each periodical successively. Collate it, and see if any abnormalities need attention. Note them at the top of the back of the front cover. Put all such cases aside in the deferred tray. If it is normal, pull out its register-card. If it is not a duplicate copy, make the necessary entry in the register-card. Taking the class number from the register-card, write it near the right hand top corner of the front cover of the periodical.

If the issue is not the one immediately after the one last registered, the entry should not be made in the next vacant horizontal line but in the line that would be appropriate to it. Write a reminder card for the earlier issue not received and put it in the week's current box for despatch. If it is a gift periodical and if an acknowledgement is due, write out the acknowledgement and put it in the week's current box. If the title-page, contents, and index are due but have not come, write a reminder card for them also and put it into the week's current box. Stamp on the covers, on all the plates and on the first and the last pages of the periodicals registered and enter the date of receipt on the cover.

Vigilance

As soon as a periodical is registered, pick out its check-card. It should be found among the cards lying behind the current week's guide. Transfer it to behind the guide-card of the week in which the next issue is due.

For example, if we are now in the first-week of March, the current week's guide-card will be 3.1. If the periodical is a weekly, the check-card should be transferred to behind the guide-card 3.2. If the periodical is a monthly, the check-card should be transferred to behind the guide-card 4.1. If the periodical is a quarterly, the guide-card should be transferred to behind the guide-card 6.1, and so on. If the check-card is not found behind the guide-card 3.1, lookup the register-card for the date on which the preceding issue was registered. Add the period of the periodical to the number of that week. The result will show the guide-card behind which the check-card could be found.

Notifying

On the last day of the week for each of the check-cards still lying behind the guide-card of the week, write out a reminder card. Fill up in each check-card the details about the reminder. Then transfer all the check-cards to behind the next week's guide-card.

Display

If any sheet in any of the periodicals registered is loose, fix it up. The Laws of Library Science require that all the periodicals should be promptly registered and displayed for the use of the public. A compact display table for periodicals was designed by me in 1937. It is now being widely used all the world over. It adds to cleanliness and strength without taking away the distinctive look of each periodical if it is encased in a plastic cover now available in all suitable sizes with Libraco Company of England. Otherwise, leave the periodical as it is without any cover. Arrange the periodicals in the classified sequence.

Take them to the display-table. In the case of each, take out the preceding number lying on it and insert the current one. All the older numbers collected in this way should be distributed in the loose-numbers-shelf, so that they may be readily available for consultation.

Rounding-off

Completion of Volume

As soon as the title-page and index are received for a volume of a periodical, register it, collect together all the issues covered by the title-page and index, collate them, and bundle them up. At the end of the week get accessioned and catalogue each completed volume of a periodical that the library has decided to keep permanently.

Faulty Cases

All faulty cases due to wrong delivery, defects found in cumulation, duplication, and all other cases should be attended to each week.

Payment of Subscription

As a routine, every week collect the bills received for payment of periodicals. For each bill examine the register-card. See if the subscription has not been paid already. See also if the claim is for the correct amount. Certify in the bill that the amount may be paid. It will be good to have a rubber stamp for it with the headings:

1. Volume last paid;
2. Date of last payment;
3. Amount of last payment;
4. Volume for which claimed;
5. Amount claimed; and
6. Explanation of discrepancy if any.

As soon as payment is sanctioned, note on the register-card, the voucher-number and its date.

Accessioning

As soon as a cumulated volume is accessioned, note the accession number in the registration card against the number of the volume.

Cumulative Index

Scan through the pages of the periodicals received, for announcement of cumulative index. If any such index is announced, take steps to order for it.

Loose Numbers

Lending of loose numbers of periodicals or newspapers is not generally allowed in public libraries. However, we have found a tendency in the libraries of many of the developed countries to lend out current issues of periodicals after they had been on the display-table for at least one week in the case of weeklies and for one month in the case of monthlies and periodicals of longer periodicity.

Forms and Registers

Renewal order card. Printed. 8 point type. Bristol board. White. The text of the form is as follows:

> Reference: This office standing order No... *dated*... Kindly renew, on behalf of the... library the subscription to... for volume/ year... and send your bill in duplicate for payment as usual

Register-card. Printed. 6 point type. Bristol board. White. 7 lines in the front page and 14 lines in the back. Gift cases, black border. Back side, column headings only.

Binding peculiarities slip. Manuscript. Ledger paper. White. The row headings in the form are as follows:

1. Title
2. Volume number
3. Year
4. Class number
5. Covering material
6. Clubbing or splitting peculiarities, if any
7. Assembling peculiarities, if any

TC I Reminder card. Printed. 8 point type. Bristol board. White. The text of the form is as follows:

> have to inform you that the Title Page; Contents, and Index to Vol.... of the... have not yet been received here. Kindly despatch them at an early date.

Non-supply card. Printed. 8 point type. Bristol board. White. The text of the form is as follows:

I have to inform you that No... of Vol... of the... was the last part received. Kindly bring the supply up to date and send future parts is issued.

Gap-in-supply card. Printed. 8 point type. Bristol board. White. The text of the form is as follows:

I have to inform you that N ... of Vol... of the... has not yet been received though a subsequent part is to hand. Kindly fill up the gap in supply at an early date,

Standing order form. Stencil. 21 lb printing paper. White. The text of the form is as follows:

Subject: Periodical Publication Order

Please supply to this library the undermentioned periodical publication. The supply is to begin from the first issue of Vol... Year ... Each issue is to be supplied promptly as and when published. The title-page, contents, and index relating to each completed volume should be supplied as soon as they are published.

The non-receipt of an issue, if any, will be notified either immediately on receipt of the latter issue or within three months after its duo date, when it is known to us. The cost of a volume is to be recovered by sending a bill in duplicate in advance, after the completion of the volume and supply of the tide-page, contents, and index.

This may be treated as a standing order until countermanded.

Weekly diary. It should have the following headings:

1. to 22 same as for S 25 of Book Order Section
2. Order cards checked
3. Orders issued
4. Volumes made up
5. Binding slips written
6. Accession cards written
7. Made up volumes transmitted
8. Accession numbers noted
9. Cumulative indexes ordered
10. Cumulative indexes received
11. Bills passed

Daily receipt diary. It is to show the number of periodical publications received from day to day. Its headings must consist of the symbols for the main divisions of classification system used or some suitable modification of them.

Files

Name		*Class Number*	*Filing Characteristic*
Standing vendors	31	(Subject device)	Vendor
Sources, enquiries and quotations	32	do	Title
Indent	33	do	do
Current periodicals	34	do	do
Finance	36	do	Correspondent
Back volumes	37	do	Title
Outward enquiries	391	do	Correspondent
Inward enquiries	392	do	do

The files are to be transferred to the record sequence one year after it is closed. The records may be destroyed after five years.

ACCESSIONING

Accession and Donation Number

Every volume to be included in the stock of the library must receive a serial number called Accession Number. Donated books must receive a Donation Number, in addition to the accession number. Cumulated volumes of periodicals should also receive accession numbers and if necessary also donation numbers, if the volume is to be bound and preserved in the library.

Accession Numbering

As soon as the classification and cataloguing of books and completed volumes of periodicals to be preserved are finished, arrange the purchased books in the sequence of their entry in their related bills, and the periodicals and the donated books in the sequence of their call numbers. Use the order cards of the purchased books as their accession cards.

Write green and red accession cards for donated books and for periodical publications respectively. Arrange also the related shelf-register cards, the accession cards, and the catalogue cards in an exactly parallel sequence. Look up the accession cabinet for the last accession and donation numbers which had been already given. Starting with the next numbers, assign the accession number, and donation number if warranted, in correct numerical sequence in each of the shelf-register cards, the accession cards, and the main catalogue cards.

Numbering the Books

Then copy the accession number, and also donation number in the case of gifted books, class number, book number, one below the other on the back of the title-page of each book. The collection symbol also should be written. The class number should begin just half an inch below the central line of the back of the title-page. If that place happens to be printed over, start it as near that place as possible. If the book has no title-page write these numbers on the top of the first page leaving space for at least two lines between the top-edge of the book and the call number.

Write these numbers also at a certain other conventional place in the book.

Passing of Bill

As soon as the writing of the numbers of the purchased books is over, write the accession number against the respective items in the bills for the purchased books. Strike off the items not supplied or rejected and make the consequential changes in the total amount of the bills. Then pass the bills for payment with the remarks "Brought into stock register. Bill may be paid."

Accession Register

On receiving accession numbers, the order cards attain the status of accession cards. File all the accession cards in the sequence of their accession numbers in the accession cabinet. This must be kept under lock and key, as these cards constitute the basic record of the books in the library, giving, as it were, a complete history of the respective books.

Further details of this routine and the complications which may arise are discussed in next chapter of *Library administration.*

Diary

Accession diary (Weekly) to show the numbers of volumes accessioned. Column headings should be: Accessioned, Donated, Purchased, Periodicals, Books.

PREPARATION OF THE BOOKS

The books themselves should be prepared. Ease the back by opening the book somewhere in the middle, placing it on a fiat table and gently running the thumb from the top to the bottom along the inner margin, working your way through the book to the two covers, turning a few leaves at a time, and simultaneously pressing. As the glue at the back of the volume is likely to have hardened, this easing work has to be done in a very careful and gentle way, so that the back of the book does not break.

Cutting Open

Cut open the pages with a cutting bone and not with a finger or a pencil as the latter will spoil the edges and even damage the text in books with narrow margins.

Stamping

Then put the library stamp, without disfiguring printed matter, in certain conventional pages such as the lower half of the half-title-page, the lower half of the back of title-page, the top of the first chapter, the bottom of the earliest chapter that ends after the fiftieth page, the bottom of the last page, each map, plate, etc and so on.

Tagging

After the stamping is over, stick a tag on the back (spine) of the volume. If there is a jacket, remove it temporarily for this purpose and replace it after the tagging is over. Apply tag exactly 2-5 cm above the bottom of the book. It will be convenient to have a piece of metal, 1.5 cm wide and bent at right angles with each of the arms exactly 2.5 cm long to mark the position for applying the tag. If the volume is too thin to have the tag on its spine, fix it on the front cover close to the spine, adjacent to the position it should have occupied on the back. Write the call number on the tag.

Date-Labelling

As soon as tagging is over, fix the date-label to the volume. The date-label is to be gummed only at the top and bottom corner of the left edge and it is to be fixed on the very first page after the cover, whether that page is an end-paper, half-title page, or even the first page of the text. Then write the book-ticket and insert it into the pocket at the bottom of the date-label. Enter the call number, accession number, and the date of release on the date-label. Now the book is ready to reach its destiny — which is reader's hand — and to rest on the shelves of the library when not solicited by readers.

Classification and Cataloguing

As it has been already indicated in section "Accession Numbering", classification and cataloguing is done even before the book is accessioned. But, the preparation work mentioned in sections "Easing" and "Date-Labelling" should be done only after accessioning is done. All this work should be done on a weekly basis like most other work in a library. Every attempt should be made to round off the week's work without any arrears.

This work will require constant use of the library catalogue. It is therefore necessary that, in addition to the catalogue in cards for public use, there should be a copy of it in slips for office use.

Process Slip

Insert in each volume a process slip, i.e., a slip 125 × 75 mm. Even a waste slip with one side blank will do. On this slip various notes regarding the volume should be entered.

Ultimately this process slip will have to be used for preparing the monthly statement of amendments to the Classification Code and the Catalogue Code and destroyed thereafter. Draw a vertical line dividing the length of the slip exactly into two parts. Reserve the left hand side for noting cross references. Divide the right hand half into three compartments by three horizontal lines. Use the first compartment to indicate class index entries, not requiring consolidation, the second to indicate cross reference index entries, the third to indicate the book index entries or main entries or class index entries. Any further notes which arise in the course of classification and cataloguing should be entered in this slip.

Classification—Routine

Sort rapidly by their main classes the volumes to be accessioned in the week. Then decide the class number of the books one by one. If any volume is elusive and requires detailed study, or appears to call for the creation of a new class, put it aside temporarily in the group of deferred volumes. For normal books, determine the call number and write it at the leading line of the process slip. Add the appropriate sequence number wherever necessary. By examining the main slip in the office-copy of the catalogue, see that the class number you give is consistent with the old placings. If there is any catalogue slip in the same ultimate class and with the same book number as the volume on hand, add the appropriate digit as the accession part of the book number. In cases of doubt compare the old books with the new ones.

Note down on the process slip notes for cataloguing work. As soon as each volume is thus treated, pass it on with the process slip for cataloguing. After all the normal volumes are dealt with take up the more difficult volumes and proceed with them when the catalogue cards of the other volumes are being written.

Amendments Noting

If any addition or amendment is made either to the rules or the schedules in the Classification Code, note them down in the official interleaved copy of the Classification Code.

Source-Slips

If any source outside the volumes classified and outside the common reference books is used in determining the class number, note it down with details on a source-slip 125 × 75 mm. The source-slip should contain in successive sections the call number of the volume classified, the call number of the source, the heading of the source, its short title, and the exact page reference. All such source-slips should be filed away in a classified sequence in the source-slips tray.

Cataloguing—Routine

Sort out the classified volumes according to their cataloguing difficulties. The following groups may arise:

1. *Fresh cards group* consisting of volumes which are in familiar languages and whose process slips do not indicate consolidation of cards;
2. *Consolidation group* consisting of volumes which are in familiar languages and whose process slips indicate consolidation of cards and periodical publications;
3. *Linguistic fresh card group* consisting of volumes in unfamiliar languages which do not require consolidation of catalogue cards;
4. *Linguistic consolidation group* consisting of volumes in unfamiliar languages which require consolidation of catalogue cards; and
5. *Refractory group* consisting of volumes of unusual cataloguing peculiarities.

Deal with the first four groups first so that the maximum number of volumes can be pushed forward without any delay.

Amendments Noting

If any amendment in the Cataloguing Code is arrived at in the course of the week, note them down in the official interleaved copy of the Catalogue Code.

Sources Noting

If the data for cataloguing has been taken from any source outside the book, prepare a source-slip and file it in the source-slip tray mentioned in above paragraph.

Checking Work

All the class numbers and cataloguing entries must be carefully checked preferably by a second person, and if no second person is available, by the same person at a later time.

Typing

If the catalogue cards are handwritten, get the slips for the catalogue for office use copied out from them by typing. If the catalogue cards themselves are typewritten, the slips for the office copy may be carbon copies.

Insertion Work

After all the volumes are completed and accession numbers are written in the main cards and the shelf cards, sort out all the catalogue cards according to the nature of their entries and insert them in the cabinets containing the public catalogue. Do similarly for the slips forming the catalogue for office use.

Guide-Cards

It will be a good practice to review the guide-cards in the cabinets of the public catalogue once in a year. New guide-cards might be necessary or experience might have suggested changes in the existing guide-cards.

Correction Work

All the old volumes set aside for correction of class number or catalogue entries should be dealt with similarly.

Forms and Registers

The description of catalogue cards is usually given in books on cataloguing. The code numbers for the different types of cards are given here. They are all 125 × 75 mm.

White cards for main entries and book index entries.

C52 *Mild-pink cards* for cross reference entries and cross reference index entries.

C53 *Guide cards.*

Black-edged white cards for class index entries.

C55 *Catalogue slips.*

S52 Volumes diary (weekly). Its column headings are to be the symbols for the main classes or any modification of them, and in addition "Total number of volumes".

S53 Cards diary (weekly). Its headings are to be:

1. Main cards;
2. Cross reference cards;
3. Class index cards;
4. Book index cards;
5. Cross reference index cards;
6. Shelf register cards;
7. Total number of cards;
8. Number of periodical publication cards consolidated;
9. Number of other cards consolidated;
10. Total number of cards consolidated.

S54 Correction diary (weekly). Similar to the volumes diary.

Specification for Card Cabinet to Hold Cards, 125 ξ 75 mm

1. The card cabinet is to consist of two parts: 1 cabinet proper; and 2 a table on which the cabinet proper rests.
2. The cabinet proper is to contain 24 drawers — four columns of six drawers each.

The external dimensions of the cabinet proper are to be:

Breadth 2 ft 4½ inches. Height 2 ft 7½ inches.
Depth 1 ft 11 inches.

The planks used for the two sides, top and bottom, are to be 7/8 inch thick and that used for the back 5/8 inch thick.

The front side of the cabinet is to be partitioned by three vertical planks 7/8 inch thick and 4 inches in breadth to secure four columns of sockets and by five horizontal planks 7/8 inch thick and 3 inch in breadth to secure six rows of sockets, to contain the drawers.

The front of each socket is to be connected with the back plank of the cabinet by two cross-bearers (one on the left and one on the right) 7/8 inch thick and I inch wide.

The cross-bearers are to be provided with two brass cylinders, each 9½ inches apart over which the drawer is to slide.

3. The internal dimensions of each socket holding the drawer are to be :

   Breadth 6 inches.

   Height 4½ inches.

   Depth 1 ft 10½ inches.

4. Each drawer is to have the following internal dimensions — breadth 5 inches and depth 1 ft 8 inches. The side and back planks used for the drawer are to be ½ inch thick and only 2½ inches high. The front plank of the drawer is to be 6¼ inches in breadth and 4¼ inches in height so as to cover the socket exactly. The bottom of the drawer is to be fitted with two reepers of ¼ inch thickness and 1 inch breadth properly centered. A brass rod $^1/_6$ inch in diameter is to run right through the centre of the drawer to lock up the card contents. To the rod projecting at the front plank of the drawer is to be screwed a screw knob. A fly nut is to be screwed to the rod projecting at the back plank of the drawer. To prevent the drawer when drawn from falling out of the socket, a self-locking catch is to be fixed into the socket to the right side at a depth of 1½ inches. A notch is to be cut in

the further end of the right hand side of the drawer. The catch is to fall in that notch and lock up the drawer automatically. On the front plank of the drawer, just above the centre, a brass label holder to hold a label $1^1/_3$ inches by 1¼ inches is to be fixed. Just below the label holder a ring is to be screwed to serve the purpose of a handle to pull out the drawer. Each drawer is to be provided with an adjustable card rest (5 ′ 3 inches and 1 inch thick at the bottom and tapering towards the top) the cross section of which is to be a right angled triangle, the hypotenuse forming the front side over which the cards should rest. The card rest is to be provided with a hole in its centre through which the central rod of the drawer is to pass. The card rest is also to be provided with a bolt so that it may be bolted to the left side plank of the drawer where holes are to be provided at intervals of 1 inch.

5. Locking arrangement of the cabinet: The vertical plank between the first and second columns of drawers and that between the third and fourth columns are to be provided with two U shaped rings each 1 ft 7½ inches apart. Two brass plates 2 inches wide and 2 ft 2½ inches long with two rectangular holes each, at required intervals to take in the U rings are to be applied to the U rings to lock up the cabinet. Four locks (one to each U ring) are to be used for locking.
6. The table on which the cabinet rests is to have the following dimensions:

   Height of the table I ft 10¼ inches (including the top plank).

   The dimensions of the top plank are to be in breadth 2 ft 5¼ inches and in depth (the side corresponding to the depth of the cabinet) 2 ft.

Thickness of the plank 7/8 inch.

The dimensions of the frame work of the table (excluding the plank) are to be 2 ft 4** inches × 1 ft 11 inches.

Legs, at the top, 3x3 inches. Legs, at the bottom, 2½ × 2½ inches.

7. The wood used for the cabinet is to be well-seasoned teakwood.
8. The contractor is to be responsible for any crack that the cabinet may develop within a year of supply.
9. The cabinet is to be coated with wood oil.
10. The cabinet is to be delivered at the Library, free of delivery charges.
11. The metal portion of the cabinet is to be of well-tempered brass.
12. The dimensions of the drawers and the sockets, and of the cabinets, as a whole, are to be quite exact so that the drawers of the cabinets may be interchanged among themselves and with the drawers of the cabinets of the specifications already in the library without any difficulty whatever.

MAINTENANCE WORK

It is pertinent to note that books should be arranged on the shelves so as to fulfil the Fourth Law of Library Science, viz, "Save the time of the reader". Reference books like encyclopaedias, dictionaries, current yearbooks and directories, and recent additions should be located in a prominent place as near the entrance as possible so that those who come for ready-reference alone may do so quickly and without disturbing the serious readers. The arrangement of the other books in the stack-room itself requires special skill. The arrangement cannot be permanent in the changing library world. It will have to be judiciously varied and readjusted from time to time. Several factors will have to be examined from time to time for this purpose.

One would very much like to have the books and periodicals arranged in the sequence of the subjects in the schedule of classification for the mere satisfaction of having them arranged in strict accordance with the schedule sequence. But the standard helpful sequence of the main classes found in the schedules of classification is seldom strictly parallel to the popular sequence. Nor is the popular sequence a permanent one. It does and must change with time.

Formation of Collections

Hence, the rigid arrangement of main classes by their numbers results in wasting the time and energy, not only of the reading public, but also of the reference staff. In an arrangement like this, a majority of readers may have to waste their time and energy in walking unnecessarily great distances to get at their books. The reference staff also are affected in the same way, as their movement is dependent on the movement of the readers. It is quite necessary to break the schedule-sequence and judiciously repermute the main-classes on the shelves.

For example, literature, as the most popular subject attracting the greatest number of readers, may be located as near the entrance as possible, irrespective of its proper place in accordance with the schedule of classification. Other subjects may be arranged at distances from the entrance varying inversely with their popularity. Any one arrangement should not be considered as final (merely on the ground of unwillingness to undertake additional labour). Use utility must be constantly tested by experience in the light of the statistics of issue. Any reshuffling of subjects found to be necessary should be immediately carried out even at the cost of additional labour and time, as the convenience of the readers is the convenience of the library.

Multiplication of Collections

The collection of books of current interest may be called the Main Collection. There may be a second collection consisting of periodicals and serials and a third one made of books of archaic interest and hence of comparatively infrequent demand. These may be called Secondary and Tertiary Collections respectively. A suitable symbol may be put above the class number of a book in all but the main collection to indicate the collection to which it belongs. Such a collection symbol may not be necessary in a bound volume of periodical, as its very look will show that it is a periodical.

Again, certain types of books, if they are put in open access shelves, are likely to be adversely affected by their being mal-handled by a few black sheep to such an extent that they are of no use to others who really want them. In this category we may include Fine Arts books, books full of art plates, and books of pornographic interest. Such books may be kept in a non-open-acceess or closed collection (not necessarily in closed shelves). By a closed collection is meant that readers will not normally be allowed to have direct or open access to the shelves containing it, but will obtain their books in most cases by the old application slip system. This restriction may be waived in the case of certain classes of responsible readers. This closed collection arrangement gives us control over the use of these books. Fine Arts books will be exposed to loss of plates if they are placed in the open access shelves. Similarly all pages savouring of obscenity are systematically purloined (to satisfy the morbid curiosity of the black sheep) from otherwise scientific treatises. A monumental example of this in the Madras University Library was Havelock Ellis" *Psychology of sex*. Previous to its withdrawal from circulation, it was in so much demand that it was treated as a reference book and kept on the issue counter. Every other reader would ask for "Ellis". Such books also should be taken over to the closed collection. Such a closed sequence may be called a Special Collection. Their book numbers may be put between two horizontal parallel lines to indicate their location.

Abnormal Size Collection

To come to the actual arrangement of books on the shelves, it is quite necessary to see that the shelves present an aesthetic appearance. This presentable appearance is of extreme importance in an open access library; for, the first thing that creates a good impression in a reader is the trim condition of the shelves with sufficient direction guides, bay guides, and shelf guides. It is a most unsightly thing in a library to see on the shelves giants, pygmies, and weaklings, all in a conglomeration minus the respect due to their ordinal arrangement. Hence, all volumes which, on account of their size and weight, preclude easy handling should be kept in a separate collection — this may be called Oversize Collection. The bottom-most plank throughout the book-racks may be used for this collection. To indicate their location, their book numbers may be overlined. Pamphlets and miniature volumes may be kept in a closed collection. This may be called Pamphlet Collection or Undersize Collection. Their location may be indicated by the underlining of their book numbers. If this is not done, such volumes invariably get themselves squeezed and even lost, either amidst other volumes or in the pockets of book-vandals.

Temporary Collections

The above mentioned sequences by no means exhaust the collections to be maintained in a growing library. While these sequences are of a permanent nature, need is felt for the formation of certain temporary sequences.

Correction Collection

If the library makes any attempt whatever to keep itself abreast of the times, there will be constant need to revise the class numbers assigned to the books in stock, in the light of the experience gained in serving the books to the readers and in consequence of the realignment and reorientation of the divisions of knowledge brought about now and then in the learned world. Change in cataloguing policy, which should be occasionally necessary, may require the revision of the catalogue entries of certain books. When groups of books are segregated for correction of class number or catalogue, they have always a tendency to stay for long, away from the stack-room. Special steps have to be taken to call for them at systematic intervals. It is better to make a separate collection of them. This may be called Correction Collection.

Binding Collection

Another factor which calls for a temporary collection is one of necessary occurrence in a popular library, which gets its books well-used and well-thumbed. As the books get worn out by such legitimate use, it fails to the lot of the Maintenance Section to play the role of the family doctor to such books. At the right time, the Maintenance Section is to send such books to the hospital on medical leave. The process of relieving them, keeping them in mind when they are patients in the bindery, and reclaiming them promptly when their treatment is over, is best regulated by looking upon them as forming a Temporary Collection, called the Binding Collection.

Here again, it is likely that more than one monthly batch will be in the hospital simultaneously. The binding collection should therefore have a number of sub-collections. It may also be wise to have their call numbers re-examined and reshaped before they are sent away to the bindery, as they are likely to have their call numbers marked permanently on their back in glittering letters of gold when they come back hale and healthy from their sojourn in the bindery.

Topical Collection

Apart from finding for every reader his book and for every book its reader, the Reference Section has also to satisfy the Fourth Law, viz, "Save the time of the reader". In certain situations, the Reference Section can achieve maximum result in this matter, if and only if the co-operation of the Maintenance Section is forth coming. This co-operation, the Maintenance Section can and should easily offer. One of the vital reasons for maintaining the shelf register in cards on the basis of "one volume, one card", is the extreme mobility that it gives to the arrangement of books.

The Maintenance Section should exploit this mobility for the benefit of the readers by freely forming Special Temporary Collections to meet the special demands that may arise from time to time. A few concrete examples will make this clear. When a special course of lectures on educational experiments was being delivered to a large class of teachers, the syllabus of the lectures was perused in advance. In consultation with the lecturer, all the books in the library, with a bearing on the course of lectures were assembled together, and put in a special cup-board as a special temporary collection dubbed Educational Experiments Lecture Collection. The Principle of Parallel Movement enabled the Maintenance Section to form such a sequence and have easy control over it, thus enabling the Reference Section to serve the teachers attending the lectures with the least loss of time. Apart from the saving of time, the psycholo gical effect was felt to be much more vital. The data on which a topical collection may be broken up may be written on the date-label and encircled.

Occasion for Topical Sequence

Every class of library, which wants to function up, will find occasion to form such Topical Collections from time to time. Local festivals, local celebrations and, any other important local event will give the occasion to the library to form such temporary topical collections. The discussion of a Bill or any momentous resolution that may come up before the legislature may prove to be an occasion to form such a temporary topical collection.

The rush of enquirers and the pressure of time in a Legislative Council Library would make the work of the librarian inefficient, if not impossible, if such temporary topical collections are not intelligently sensed and formed in advance and, their formation would be impossible even if they are sensed, but for the extraordinary power which is given to him by this wonderful invention, by the library profession, of this extremely mobile shelf-register-in-cards, and the equally facile Principle of Parallel Movement. Perhaps, the value of the freedom to form such temporary topical collections at pleasure will be most appreciated in business localities, whose patrons know best the value of time and indeed look upon time as money and money as time.

Principle of Parallel Movement

Having been obliged to disturb the schedule sequence and to arrange the books in so many collections, it is a great responsibility for the Maintenance Section to maintain correct sequence in the shelves and to see that every book is in its correct place. The mechanical apparatus invented by the library profession to cure this is what is known as the Shelf Register. It is made up of cards of standard size, viz, 125 × 75 mm, written on the principle — one title, one card — with the call number in the leading line. These shelf register cards are kept absolutely parallel to the books on the shelves, which means that they are to be arranged in an equal number of collections. What is more, except when the books leave their proper place on the shelves to get into the hands of a reader, every movement of the books should be controlled and imitated by an exactly parallel movement among the shelf register cards.

The discovery of this Principle of Parallel Movement has turned out to be panacea of most of the ills in the management of the books in the library and brought in its train the inevitable genesis of the Maintenance Section. The shelf register cabinet is the hub of the stock in the library and correspondingly the Maintenance Section is the hub of the staff of the library.

Guides

The Maintenance Section should put up guide-boards to places like reading room, periodicals room, catalogue room, stack-room, etc so that readers can by themselves find their way about in the library.

Within the stack-room itself, there should be tier-guides and gangway-guides showing the subjects in the respective tiers and gangways. There should also be bay-guides in each bay showing the subjects contained in it. It has been found from experience that each bay-guide may have to be in at least six lines. All the above mentioned guides may consist of thick card boards 35 × 12 cm coveted with white paper. Each bay, whose standard width is about 1 m will require two guides. The legends, which should consist of the class numbers and their equivalent in the natural language, may be stencilled on these guide-boards. Each shelf-plank also should have shelf guides. As the standard length of a shelf-plank is about 1m, it is found helpful to have an average of three shelf-guides in a plank. These shelf-guides may be strips 125 × 12mm cut from white Bristol boards.

Discarded catalogue-cards with one side blank may be used for cutting these strips. The shelf-guide also should give the class number and its equivalent in the natural language. Since we have said that on an average there will be one shelf-guide for every 25 cms of shelf-plank, it is obvious that in a stack-room accommodating 25,000 volumes, about 3,000 shelf-guides will be needed. It is not an easy matter to maintain these shelf-guides. As the books will be frequently moving forward as a result of new accessions, these shelf-guides also will have to be frequently moved forward and adjusted. This will add to the task of maintaining the shelf-guides. The best way of facilitating this work is to provide wedge-shaped grooves along the front edge of shelf-plank in which the shelf-guides can be slided.

It must be a matter of prestige for the Maintenance Section that no guide tells a wrong tale. The shelf-guides will have to be carefully watched and adjusted, from time to time, into their proper position. The bay-guides may not require such frequent attention. But whenever books have to be transferred from one bay to another the bay-guides should be immediately corrected. The gangway-guides and the tier-guides will not require even as much renewal as the bay-guides.

To take away from the monotony of the appearance of shelf-arrangement, to exploit the Principle of Novelty, to help every book to get its reader, and to keep step with the slowly changing scale of popularity of subjects with the reading public, it will be desirable to reshuffle the disposition of the subjects in the stack-room at suitable intervals. Once in five years the whole library may have to be reshuffled. Every year some particular region may have to be reshuffled. Whenever such wholesale re-arrangement takes place, the bay-guides and the gangway-guides will have to be mostly re-written.

Renewal of Tags

The tags on the backs of books should be rapidly reviewed each day. The entire stack-room should be covered in this way at least once in a month. During this review, all worn-out tags should be replaced by fresh ones and the call numbers copied on them. All the newly written call numbers should be verified by somebody else or by the same person on the next day before the volumes are back on the shelves.

Open Access Without Guides

It is sheer callousness to adopt open access system without plenty of guides, or even if there are guides, to leave the guides unchanged in an ever-changing library. It will be frustration to readers. It will even irritate them. It will bring odium on the library staff. There is no doubt that maintenance of plenty of guides in their right places will consume considerable staff-time. Library authorities should take this into account in providing staff. But on the side of the staff also, they should have a sense of value which is sufficiently compelling to make them feel miserable even if one guide is in the wrong place or one plank is without guides.

New Books

The work of absorbing the accession of the week into the stock should be done on a weekly basis. As soon as the preparation of the new volumes of the week is over, sort them out according to their collections. In each collection arrange the volumes by their call numbers. Do similarly for their shelf-cards. Taly them. Books of a normal nature fit for display in the recent additions shelf should now be separated with a parallel separation of shelf-cards. These separated shelf-cards should be put ha the recent additions box behind the guide "Collection 0". Take this box and the new volumes to the recent additions shelf which should be in the first row of shelves in the stack-room. Pull out all the volumes corresponding to the shelf-cards behind the guide "Collection 2" As each volume is pulled out, turn its shelf-card in its own plane through a right angle so that it stands on its shorter edge. If any volume is not to be found, trace it out. Alter all the books have been traced out, transfer the guide-card "Collection 1" to the place where the guide-card "Collection 0" is, transferring the latter to the end of the current week's cards. Put the current week's books, meant for display, on the recent additions shelf in the classified sequence.

Released Books

Hand over to the counter all the released books which have been bespoken. Take the remaining books along with the other books of the current week and shelve them in their proper places. Take out from the recent additions box the shelf-cards which are standing on their shorter edges and put them along with the shelf-cards of the week's additions which are not to be put on the recent additions shelf. File these cards in the proper places in the shelf-register cabinet.

Used Books

Consulted Books

Every hour, walk round the reading room and collect the books left by readers on their respective tables after consultation. Enter the statistics in the consultation counting sheet and shelve the books in the returned-books-shelf in a roughly classified sequence. This shelf may be in the first row of shelves in the stack-room.

Borrowed Books

The books returned by members at the discharging counter should also be brought to the returned-books-shelf at convenient intervals and shelved in a roughly classified sequence.

Replacing

Readers should be allowed to take away for consultation on loan any books lying in the returned-books-shelves. There is no gain in segregating them and keeping them away from the use of readers until they go back to their permanent places in the stack-room. On the other hand since the books in the replaced-books-shelves will be popular ones, there is every chance that many of them will go into reader's hand in the course of the day and that the books to be actually replaced will be considerably reduced in number — resulting in the saving of the time of the staff. But the volumes which stay back in the returned-books-shelf should be replaced in their permanent places once in a day at an appointed hour. This hour should be the slackest hour in the library.

Correction

For all the volumes taken out for correction work, transfer the shelf-cards to behind the correctly dated guide-cards in the correction collection. When these volumes come back after correction, shelve them in their proper places and file their shelf-cards also in a parallel manner. Periodically the shelf-cards in the correction collection should be checked and steps should be taken to round off the work without undue delay.

Rectification and Verification

In an open access library, readers are never allowed to replace books on the shelves. They have freedom only to pick out books from the shelves. In spite of this convention, books do get mixed up as a result of the reader's browsing round the stack-room. Even apart from criminally-minded people deliberately putting a book in quite a distant place, the unintended misplacements within the same shelf-planks would in the long run mount to very near chaos. Unless the books are put back in proper sequence periodically, readers will be put to much difficulty; nor can the library staff find books easily. The process of restoring order among the books is called Shelf-Rectification. There is also need for periodical Stock-Verification. This is normally done once in a year. This practice usually involves much disturbance in the rhythm of the work of the library. Some libraries go to the criminal extent of closing down to the public for the period of stock-verification. This practice violates all the Laws of Library Science . The necessary shelf-rectification and stock-verification can be combined into a single process. In other words stock-verification will be automatically done not merely once in a year but even more than once if shelf-rectification is properly designed and correctly carried out.

All the regions of a library may not be equally prone to disturbance by readers. The main collection will be the most disturbed. The closed collection will not be disturbed at all. The secondary and the tertiary collections will be disturbed much less than the main one. It is desirable that shelf-rectification should be done in the main collection at least once in a month. That for the secondary collection may perhaps be done once in six months. It may be enough to attend to the other collections once in a year. But, the frequency of periodical dusting and cleaning of these collections should be in just the reverse sequence. This is because in the main collection the books are constantly disturbed by the readers themselves and dust and insects cannot therefore accumulate very much. But in the other collections they will accumulate.

The daily quota of the region for shelf-rectification can be arrived at by taking the total length of shelving to be rectified and the period in which it should be done. Each day, take out the shelf-register trays for the day's quota. As far as possible make the end-points of the quota the end-points of convenient subjects. The rectification-work should be done by two people.

One of the persons should read out, from the charged tray at the counter, the call numbers of all the book-cards lying within the range of the day's quota. As each call number is read out, the second person should turn its shelf-card through a right angle in its own plane so as to stand on its shorter edge.

Do similarly for all the books of the concerned region, lying in the bespoken collection or among the books returned or being consulted by readers.

Final Checking

Then take the trays to the region of the stack-room to be checked. One person should go on reading the call numbers of the books on the shelves. The other person should go on looking up and pushing towards himself, the corresponding shelf-register cards. If any shelf-register card standing on its shorter edge intervenes, it must be turned down to its normal position. If the book corresponding to any shelf-card lying in the normal position is not read out by the man at the shelf, that shelf-card should be turned so as to stand on the shorter edge. The result will be that at any moment the cards that stand on the shorter edge in the checked region will be those of untraced books. On the other hand the cards which stand on the shorter edge in the unchecked region will be those of traced books. As the checking proceeds, misplaced books will happen to be read out by the man at the shelf. It may happen that the card of a misplaced book is found standing on its shorter edge in the checked region. It may then be restored to its normal state of standing on the longer edge. It may also happen, that the shelf-card of a misplaced book is in the unchecked region of the tray. If so, ask the man at the shelf to shelve the book at the proper place. If any reader takes away a book of the unchecked region of the day's quota, before he leaves the region, the shelf-card of the book may be turned so as to stand on its shorter edge. Thus there will be no obstruction whatever for readers to use any book they like when the shelf-rectification *cum* stock-verification is proceeding. As soon as the checking of the day's quota is over, enter in the investigation note-book the details of the cards standing vertically on their shorter edges; and then restore the cards to their normal position. Insert the shelf register tray in its proper place.

Untraced Books

Investigate the items untraced with the aid of the investigation note-book. As each item is traced, restore it to its proper place and strike out the entry in the investigation note-book. The items that do not get traced out within the year should be taken as lost books.

Speed of Rectification

Experience has shown that, if the classification scheme used is an individualising one like the Colon Classification with the book number designed in an organic relation to the class number, it is sufficient if the book number alone is read out All that is needed is to have an occasional check-up by reading the whole class number. Even the occasions for it are automatically indicated when some difficulty arises. The number for the book numbers on the backs of books alone to be strictly parallel to the book numbers in the shelf-cards without the class numbers also being strictly parallel, is negligibly small. This makes shelf-rectification expeditious. Nearly a thousand volumes can be done in an hour. This means that by doing shelf-rectification work for one hour a day a cycle of 25,000 volumes can be checked in a month. The main collection in most of the public libraries is not likely to exceed 25,000 volumes.

Binding

An important part of maintenance work is to keep the books in a physically fit condition. The standard of artistic binding of books for private use — which means very sparing use — is quite high. But re-inforced library binding to stand constant wear and tear has not yet come into vogue in India. Even concepts like split boards and French joints are unknown. The necessary materials of good quality are not easily available. It is therefore necessary that the most detailed specification should be given for library binding. It would be a good policy to ask the binder to take personal instruction from the librarian. A specification of library binding is given at the end of this chapter for ready reference. Each library should also train some member of the staff to make petty repairs. A stitch in time saves nine, as the saying goes.

Damaged Books

The damaged books should be picked up by the circulation staff and segregated for attention. It is also desirable to walk round the stack-room and pull out books needing re-binding. All the cumulated volumes of periodicals intended to be preserved will require to be bound. It is again a matter of policy whether a book should be sent to the bindery after the publishers' case is worn out or even at the beginning before it is released for circulation. We are of the opinion that the life of the book will be considerably lengthened if the latter course is adopted.

If we can get books from publishers unbound in sheets, it is well and good. In Norway where few publishers agree to do so, we found that the Director of Libraries ruthlessly pealed off the publishers' cases as soon as the books arrived from the publishers. He even employed a fairly large staff to do this pealing work ! In any case books in paper covers should not be released for the use before being bound. At the same time every book may not need costly library binding. In the case of books of passing interest, particularly ordinary fiction, usually printed on bad paper, it may be cheaper to buy additional copies than to have them bound in the library style.

Perhaps binding work is best done on a monthly basis. As soon as the quota for the month has been collected, arrange them in a classified sequence. Take out their shelf-register cards and form a binding collection of them. Scrutinize the volume from the point of view of their binding peculiarities and form them into homogenous groups. Arrange the volumes in each such group in classified sequence. Prepare binding slips for each of them. Make an order copy for binding from out of these slips. Ask the binder to come to the library and collate all the volumes. If any volume is defective, decide whether it is worth binding. If it is, note the defects in its binding slip. Hand over the volumes to the binder. Keep the slips in the *binding box*.

Bound Volumes

Before forwarding begins — that is, before the covering material is applied — inspect the books in the bindery to see if the specification has been fully followed. When the bound volumes come back to the library, check them with the binding slips, scrutinise if the tooling has been properly done, insert the books in their proper places, merge the corresponding shelf cards in their proper places, and check the binder's bill with regard to style of binding and the rates claimed.

Specification for Reinforced Library Binding

Assembling

Collation. All books received by the contractor are to be examined and collated and any found to be imperfect or seriously damaged are to be returned unbound to the librarian. Torn leaves and plates are to be neatly repaired.

A periodical shall not be held to have been collated properly nor to be perfect, unless all the parts of a volume are bound in correct order of pagination and the usual title and contents pages and indexes are inserted in the proper places. Unless each imperfect and damaged book is reported upon to the librarian and unless the librarian has instructed the contractor to proceed with the work on such books, the bill will not be paid for any such books bound or repaired.

Wrappers and advertisements in periodicals and books are to be bound in, if the contractor is instructed to do so; otherwise, they are not to be bound in.

Stitching

Sewing. Books printed on paper of good quality are to be sewn one sheet on (except where thinness of paper makes it necessary to sew two sheets on) with unbleached thread of suitable thickness over unbleached linen tapes. Books printed on soft, spongy or brittle paper are to have the sections lined at inner and outer folds with strips of thin but tough paper before they are sewn. All sections broken at the back are to be lined with tough paper or linen strips, and where necessary neatly overcast on modern methods of cross stitching before being sewn to the tapes. The first and last sections of all books are to be enclosed at back in linen strips.

All separate leaves, plates, maps, plans, etc, are to be mounted on guards of linen or tough thin paper and to be sewn in. Pasting on is not to be permitted. Double plates are to be guarded at the fold. No charge is to be made for the first dozen plates so guarded in each book. For books up to post octavo (6¼″ × 3-$^{7}/_{8}$″) three tapes, one-quarter inch in width, are to be used. For books of crown octavo (7½″ × 5") four tapes, one-quarter inch in width, are to be used. For books of larger sizes the number of tapes and their width are to be increased in proportion. Two of the tapes are to be placed within one inch of the head and tail of each book.

Straight-line machine stitching will not be accepted.

Books printed on calendared or heavily loaded art paper are to be reported to the librarian and a quotation sent to him for lining each leaf of such books with a linen hinge on a throw-up guard.

All folded *maps and illustrations* are to be mounted on jaconet or thin linen of good quality and to be charged for separately.

End-papers. End-papers are to be of good tough opaque paper of approved mild colour, with at least one plain white leaf between each of them and the printed matter. The end-papers are to be made with strong linen or cloth joints and to be sewn on as a section.

Cutting edges. Unless otherwise instructed the contractor is to cut edges of books accurately and to take care to leave margins as wide as possible. Unless other instructions are given, the edges are to be sprinkled or tinted with a colour harmonising with the colour of the materials used for covering.

Forwarding. Unless otherwise directed, all books should

have French joints and tight or close flexible backs with the covering material attached directly to the back. Tapes are to be firmly inserted between split boards. Books bound in quarter leather or in cloth or in buckram are to have the boards slightly rounded at corners and the covering material is to be neatly folded and not mitred. Leathers are not to be unduly pared down or unduly stretched in covering. The covering material of back is to extend over boards to at least one sixth of the width of the book. All books should open up freely and lie flat.

Lettering. Lettering is to be impressed in best gold directly on to the material which covers the book. The lettering is to be of good size and easily readable; small lettering will not be accepted except on very thin books. No extra charge will be allowed up to and including fifty letters or/and figures.

Sizes. The size of a book is to be determined by the measuremeat of the board, the square of which must not exceed one-eighth of an inch in books up to crown octavo, and proportionately for larger sizes. Extra charges for thickness is to be allowed only when the thickness of the volume exceeds one half the width of its boards. No extra charge is to be made for two or more volumes bound in one, unless the thickness of such a volume exceeds one half the width of the boards. In submitting the bills for work done, the measurement of the board should be given in inches in addition to the conventional mode of specifying the size.

Alternative -suggestions. When the preceding instructions are obviously inapplicable to any book or for any reason undesirable, the contractor is to submit suggestions for binding such a book with estimate of cost.

General. The whole of the work in binding is to be carried out with due regard to the fact that the books will be subjected to hard wear and tear and that the binding is to be permanent. Special instructions, if any, given with reference to particular volumes sent for binding should be faithfully carried out.

Materials

Thread. To be of best unbleached linen of suitable thickness,

Tapes. To be of best unbleached linen, of close strong texture and of the specified width.

Glue. To be best quality flexible glue mixed with copper sulphate to keep off insects.

Boards. To be good quality mill boards.

Leathers. The contractor must guarantee or undertake to produce, when required, the guarantee of the firm supplying the leather, that all skins used

1. have been tanned in sumach or oak bark or similar vegetable stuff, or a mixture of them;
2. are free from sulphuric or other deleterious acids;
3. have been dyed with colours that are fast with respect to light as well as moisture; and
4. are genuine as described.

Buckram. To be linen buckram of best quality.

Cloth. To be good quality art canvas or imperial morocco cloth fast colour and finish.

Gold. To be best English gold.

FINANCE AND ACCOUNTS IN LIBRARIES

The task of raising money, investing funds, managing property, preparing and getting the sanctions for the budget, and all other financial matters relating to a public library usually fall to the share of the Local Body which is the Local Library Authority. Nevertheless there may be some amount of financial work that falls to the share of the library. It will have to do initial work in the framing of the budget. This will have to be done according to the standing instruction of the Local Body. So also it is in regard to accounts. We shall deal here only with the work of primary book-keeping which must be dons by the library staff and even here to confine ourselves only to what is distinctively of library nature. Matters relating to pay-bill, permanent advance, miscellaneous receipts, etc will be regulated by the standing orders prevailing in the Local Body.

Double Payment

One of the dangers to be specially watched is double, payment. As books and periodicals dribble in, all through the year, special effort is necessary to avoid double payment. Some kind of automatic check, not depending on memory is necessary. With regard to books, control by book-order-cards as described in section 423 will prove effective.

If a book arrives and there is no book-order-card for it, you should not improvise a card in order to accept the book. You must have complete trust in the cards-file. Card system of this kind can work only if every routine is carried out thoroughly and faithfully at every stage. If the card is not in the order tray, the presumption should be that the book had already arrived and that the order card had been taken out or that the book is not due on any order. It might be lying in the sequence corresponding to the current week's arrival or it might have been already converted into an accession card and filed in the proper place. In the latter case the card will show the date of payment and the number of the voucher of payment. In the case of a periodical, the routine suggested in section "Payment of Subscription" will, if faithfully carried out, prevent double payment.

Bills Register

Another danger in dealing with supplies dribbling in day after day is that certain supplies are neglected and never paid, at any rate not promptly paid. The best way to control this is to have a properly designed register of bills. As soon as bills are received, couple each bill with its duplicate if any. Group the bills by the parties to whom payment should be made. Arrange the bills in each party's group by the numbers of the order to which they relate. To make this easy the parties should be instructed never to include in any one bill supplies made relating to more than one order. Register the bills in the sequence in which they have been thus brought. Post the register number at the right hand top corner of the bill as well as it duplicate.

Arrangement of the Bills

Tie together all the bills payable to one party. Verify the total of each bill On the back of the last sheet of the bunch of bills, write the total of each of its successive sheets and total up the figures. Get the posting of the figures and the grand total verified by another person or by yourself at some later time. This must be done both for the original and for the duplicate copy of the bills.

If a bill has no duplicate, the duplicate copy must be prepared. Put the pay-order-stamp in a convenient place on the last sheet of the bunch of bills. Also at the bottom of each sheet of the bunch, put the stamp "Included in voucher number...." Write the amount in words in the imprint of the pay-order-stamp. Write the pay order inclusive of remittance charges, if any, at the end of the office copy of the bill.

Arrange the bunches in a convenient sequence according to the nature and amount of payment.

Voucher

Enter each bunch in a separate line of the register of payments in serial sequence. The serial number, got by it in the register of payments, is called Voucher-Number. Write the voucher-number in the fair copy as well as the office copy of each bunch of the bills and also at the bottom of each sheet in a bunch. Then the voucher is ready for payment. The voucher-number should begin with T at the beginning of each financial year.

Posting of Voucher-Number

It is at this stage that the voucher-numbers should be posted in all the accession cards of the books and the register cards of the periodicals concerned.

Allocation Register

It will be necessary to watch the progress of payment for books and periodicals so that the amount allocated for each subject is not exceeded. This is controlled by allocating the amount of each voucher to the different subjects under the heads "books" and "periodicals" in a special allocation register.

Forms and Registers

Bills Register. Printed. 10 point type. 21 lb printing paper. White. Bound book. Folio pagination. 30 lines per page. The text above the column headings and the column headings are to be:

(Name of library) Register of Bills Received in....

Register N of Bill (1.5 cm); Date of receipt of Bill (1.5 cm); Outside date (1.5 cm); Outside N (1.5 cm); From whom (5 cm); Purport — Books or Periodicals and main class symbols (4 cm); Amount (2.5 cm); Initials (1.5 cm); Amount (2.5 cm); Draft requisition date; initials (1.5 cm); Script N and Date (1.5 cm); Script received date; initials (1.5 cm); P. O., M..O. N (1.5 cm); Despatch date; initials (1.5 cm); Acknowledgement reminder date; initials (1.5 cm); Acknowledgement receipt date; initials (1.5 cm); Acknowledgement filing; initials (1.5 cm); Remarks.

Payments Register. (Books and Periodicals) Printed. 10 point type. Ledger paper. White. Bound book. Folio pagination 20 lines per page. The text above the column headings and the column headings are to be as follows:

> *(Name of the library)* Payment Register— Books and Periodicals [Year; Date (1.5 cm); Voucher N (1.5 cm); Bill N (1.5 cm); Bill] date (1.5 cm); Party and place (9 cm); Books (5 cm); Periodicals (5 cm); Subjects symbols (6.5 cm); Remarks.

Allocation Register. Printed. 10 point type. 21 lb printing paper. White. Bound book. Folio pagination. 30 lines per page. The text above the column headings and the column headings are to be:

> *(Name of library)* Allocation Register (Year)

Month and week (1.5 cm); Voucher N (1.5 cm); Different currencies in which payment is claimed (2.5 cm for each currency) for books; Different currencies in which payment is claimed for periodicals (2.5 cm for each periodical); Total (2.5 cm for each currency); Remarks.

Files

The call numbers for files of various kinds have been given in section 48 and at the end of sections whose numbers end with 8 previous chapter. These numbers are the same as those given in the *Library administration.* Wherever "subject device" is added after a file number, the file number should be amplified by the class number for the subject concerned. For example, 23 is the number for order files, 23R will be the number for order files relating to books in Philosophy. Similarly 34 is the class number for files relating to current periodicals. 34R will be the number for files relating to current periodicals in Philosophy. 21 is the number for files on standing vendors. 23P15 will be the number for files on standing vendors for Sanskrit Books.

BUILDING AND STORES

The main work relating to library building, equipment, stationery, and other articles needed for library use, will be looked after normally by the parent body of the library. However, the library will have some routine connected with them. Before taking up the routine, it may be worth-while to say a few words about some features which are expected in a small library building.

Building

There should be a gangway down the wall which is at least 1 m wide in the stack-rooms. This gangway will protect the book-racks from rain and sun. Further as an additional precaution it is always insisted in our country that the lengthwise wall in which these stack-room windows occur should run from east to west. The floor should be sound-proof. Either the pavement material itself should be sound-proof or if it is too costly to get such material in Indian conditions today, the floor should be covered with some matting. Coir matting may be cheap enough and within the means of many of our small libraries.

Book-Rack

The following is the specification for a unit book-rack:

That standard unit-rack that I have designed for the Madras University Library has two faces. Each face has two bays, so that the unit-rack is a four-bayed rack — two bays on each side. While the height may be 7 ft in adult libraries, it should not exceed 5 ft in children's libraries. The detailed dimensions of and specification for all adult library unit are as follows:

1. External dimensions 6' 6" ′ 1' 6" ′ 7'.
2. Three uprights, each 2" ′ 1' 6" ′ 7".
3. Seven shelf-planks, each 3' ′ 8½" ′ 1".

Two of the shelf-planks are to be fixed ones—one near the top and the other near the bottom. The other five are to be movable ones supported by Tonk's fittings, so that they can be adjusted to an inch. It may be an advantage to provide two spare shelves for each unit.

2. The book-rack is to have sanitary bottom — i.e. the lowest shelf is to be fixed at a height of 6 ins from the floor to facilitate cleaning the floor beneath the rack and easy vigilance. The topmost shelf is to be fixed 6 ins below the top of the uprights.

3. To prevent the books on the shelves in one face getting mixed up with the books on the corresponding shelves in the other face, an expanded metal or weld-mesh partition is to separate the two faces. It is to accommodate this frame that the planks are made only 8½ inches broad, thus leaving a gap of 1 inch in the centre of the rack. The partition is to begin only from a height of 6 inches from the lowest fixed shelf and go right up to the lower side of the uppermost fixed shelf. The advantage in beginning it only from a height of 6 inches from the lowermost shelf is that giant folios, which are more than a foot broad, can be made to lie flat, on

the bottom-most fixed shelves, extending from one face to the other. If the partition is of steel, it should be coated with an anti-corrosive paint.

4. The front-edge of each shelf is to have a wedge-shaped groove cut in it, to hold shelf-cards. If the groove is carefully cut, the shelf-cards can be easily slided from end to end, as the books are necessarily moved in course of time.

5. The three uprights are bound together by the four pairs of fixed shelves. It would be an advantage to re-inforce this by means of two steel tie-rods binding them together, one at a height of 2½ ft from the botton and the other at a depth of 2½ ft from the top. To accommodate these rods it may be necessary to make the partition in three parts, the rods running between the frames of the parts.

6. It may be convenient to fix spring blind-holders to each bay to hold maps. At least two maps can be accommodated in front of each bay. The maps are to be normally in the rolled-up position. Whenever necessary, they are to be pulled out for reference and then released.

7. This unit-rack requires about 10 c ft of teakwood. It has 84 running ft of shelf-space. It can accommodate, on an average, 750 volumes. When full of books, it will weigh about 1 ton.

8. The teakwood used should be well-seasoned and the contractor should make good any crack that it may develop within a year of supply. The length of all the shelf-planks should be quite accurate, so that they can be interchanged without any restriction.

Opening Routine

Before opening the main gate, go round the building and see if there is anything abnormal. Ask the night watchman about his observations in the night. Check his work. See if the lock of the main gate is intact and untampered with. Then, examine if the doors and the windows are in the proper bolted position. Then, ask the peon to open them and report to you anything abnormal that he might notice. Ask him to report also all cases of broken panels, broken bolts, hooks, etc. Then, walk through the different parts of the buildings in accordance with a systematic plan, examining if there is any defect anywhere in the electric installation.

Examine also if there is evidence of damage done by rats, bats, squirrels, and other similar creatures. Examine also if there is any sign of white ants anywhere. If there had been rain on the preceding day, examine if there, are signs of leakage anywhere. Examine if the counter wicket gates are in a sound condition and if they work properly. Examine if all the electric switches are in good working condition. As you go round, if any defects are observed, make an accurate note of the same in your diary. Soon after this proccess is over, take the necessary action about each of the defects noticed.

If anything serious is noticed, bend word to the librarian immediately. Fill up the columns relating to opening in the diary of the section. Wind the clocks and the time pieces on the due days and set them right whenever necessary.

Closing Routine

Examine if there is no person in any room or part of the building before it is closed. Ask a peon to go round and close and fix the bolts of all the doors and windows in a systematic manner. Inspect each of the doors and windows and examine if they have been securely bolted. Examine if any inflammable material is lying about loosely anywhere and if it does, have it removed. Put the bait in the rat traps and distribute the traps in the parts of the library, which are known to be frequented by rats. Rats are cunning creatures. It is our experience that we have to change the bait from time to time and also change the places where the traps are placed from time to time. In spite of all the ingenuity that man is capable of, the rodents are uncanny enough to thwart all his efforts, evade his traps and take its to'l from some other part of the library. If the building could be designed rat-proof, a good deal of this bother will be avoided. Take the diary of the section with you and turn the fans and lights off individually after satisfying yourself that nobody is left behind in any part of the library. Then, tura off the sub-main switches. Then turn off the main switch. Then, ask the peon to lock the main door securely.

- Pull it and see if it is properly locked. Ask the night watchman also to satisfy himself that it is properly locked. Then, seal it up. Then, enter the columns relating to closing, in the section's diary. Send the key and the diary to the person who is to have custody of the same during the night.

Stores

The issue of the articles is to be regulated and controlled by a combined stock and issue register. In the case of each article, the following "constants" are to be fixed from experience and suitably changed at intervals in the light of further experience:

1. Maximum to which the stock should be brought up periodically— say, once in a year, the period being determintd for each article;
2. The minimum below which the stock should not go, i.e., when the stock reaches that figure, steps should be taken for replenishment;
3. The annual consumption;
4. The quantum of issue. It will add to convenience and

economy of time, if articles are issued only in a definite number of quanta. The quantum for each article is to be determined according to its nature; for example, catalogue cards are to be issued only in quanta of 100. The indenting section should ask only for 100 cards or multiples of 100 cards. It should not ask for fractions of a quantum. The quantum for writing paper may be 100 sheets; and so on.

In the light of these figures and in the light of the frequency of issue, each article is to be given a certain number of pages in the stock and issue register so that the pages allotted to all the articles are finished off, more or less at the same time.

Apart from this standardisation of the quantum of issue, it is desirable that the issue is controlled and standardised from the point of view of time also. It is slovenly and annoying to run out of stock of stationery in the middle of work and to run out to the stores at odd hours.

Stationery Articles

Another important factor in the organisation of work regarding stores relates to the storing of the ankles. In the case of forms and registers, receptacles of suitable size and shape are necessary. The forms and registers should be arranged strictly in the sequence of their numbers as shown next chapter. The stationery and other articles should be arranged in some convenient sequence in receptacles of their own which should also be of proper size. The store-room should be kept scrupulously neat and tidy.

If the quantum principle of distribution is adopted and if the articles themselves are packed in quanta, the tidiness in storing arrangement will be easily secured. Further, the verification of stock will also be greatly facilitated. Here is a schedule of stationery which may be required in a library.

Straw board
Packing paper (60 lb)
Brown cartridge paper (46 lb)
Bristol boards, 4 sheets thick
Ledger paper 27"x 17" (for printing)
Paper (white) 21 lb 27"x 17" (for printing)
Rubber stamp ink
Stamping pad
Stencil (Alphabet and Arabic numerals)
Ruler
Twine
Thread
Paper weights
Drawing pin
Tap tag
Pin
Jem Clip
Paper clip (steel)
Drying book
Blotting paper
Flat file boards
Hinged file boards
Bound file books
Pencil (black lead)
Pencil (blue lead)
Pencil (red lead)
Pencil (phono) required for writing call numbers also
Penholder

Paper (white) 16 lb 27″ ′ 17″
Section paper
Manifolding paper
Carbon paper
Impression paper
Stencil paper
Black ink
Red ink
Paper cutter
Dhungry cloth
Umbrella
Wheat flour
Copper sulphate
Phenyle
Soap
Gum bottle
Sealing wax
Sponge
Dater
Calling bell
Typewriter
Typewriter ribbon
Typewriter eraser
Typewriter oil
Benzine oil
Typewriter metal polish
Typewriter brush
Long cloth
Duplicating machine
Duplicator ink
Duplicator obliterine
Roneo pen

Nibs	Stencil plate
Ink bottle	Lamp black
Ink stand	Candle stand
Eraser	Electric bulb
Eraser, ink (black)	Cycle, with its tools
Eraser, ink (red)	Rubber solution
Stencil ink	Cycle oil
Punch plier	Valve tube
Needle	Pump connection
Inch tape	Metal polish
Foot-rule	Grease
Knife	Match box
Scissors	Lantern
Kerosene oil	Tonk's shelf plates and other similar fittings
Polishing wax	Nail puller
Sand paper	Hammer and other tools

It is desirable that the entire stores of the library should be checked at least once in a year. The best time to check it is just before the year's supply is received.

Preventive Injuries

Fungus

A group of omnivorous fungus known as mildew or moulds is destructive of paper and leather. They are recognised by the white scars they produce. It grows much when humidity is above 70 per cent and most when it reaches 90 per cent and the temperature is between 25°C and 38°C. Ventilation controls moulds to some extent. To provide for aeration, books must be loosely arranged on shelves. In winter, steel shelves cause local lowering of temperature producing near the books pockets of more humid air.

Silver-Fish

Silver-fish has glistening silver-grey scales on the body, long antennae on the head and filaments at the hind-end. It is less than half an inch in length. It hides away all day and feeds on binding starch, and paper at night and in darkness.

Book-Worm

Book-worm is the popular name for the larva of beetles. It eats paper and leaves its eggs on the surface of binding or on the edges of books. The eggs hatch within ten days during summer. The larva eats its way into the interior of the book and reaches the surface again when ready for crysalis stage. It has about five life-cycles in a year. Its damage is recognised by the pinholes and tunnels across the leaves of books.

Foundation

When the building is erected, the earth in the site should be dug up and cleared of nests of queen-ants. The soil of the foundation trenches may be soaked with a 20 per cent solution of zinc chloride or copper sulphate. The superstructure should be isolated from foundation by a damp-proof course of concrete slate or asphalt. Stone or burnt brick and lime-mortar or cement alone should be used in construction. Floors should not have cracks or joints. Monolithic concrete should be preferred. The settlement joints and the junction of the floor with walls should be grouted with cement or plastic coal tar. This should be repeated whenever cracks develop. Another preventive against white ants is to treat joints and cracks and crevices with solution of one part corrosive sublimate and 16 parts methylated spirit. An wood-work should be of teak properly treated, for which advice may be taken from the Forest Research Institute at Dehra Dun. The stack-room may be air-conditioned. But this will not be within the reach of our small libraries. The next best is to provide for adequate ventilation, sunlight, and dryness. Napthaline bars, lime, mergosa leaf, and tobacco-leaf have preventive effect. Buckets of coal may keep humidity under control.

White Ant

White ants are perhaps the most dreadful destroyer in libraries in tropics. They live mostly on cellulose and paper and board made of it. It is the subterranean species that are most destructive in libraries. As they have a reserve of queen-ants, it is difficult to eradicate them. Like silver-fish, white ant also shuns light.

Handling of Books

Open access is the best prevention against all the above mentioned ills. In regions into which readers go often, the books are constantly handled and injurious organisms do not find harbour. In regions which contain books not much in use, books must be frequently taken out, cleaned, aired, and exposed to sunlight. Black colour should be avoided in the covering materials of the binding. Red colour has proved to attract insects least.

Files

Name		*Class Number*	*Filing Characteristic*
Indent	9972	(Last digit of the year to which the indent relates)	Correspondent
Forms	9974	(N of the form)	do
Distribution	9976	(N of the ankle)	do
Sanctioned indents	9977		
Stock verification	9978	(Last digit of the year to which the verification refers)	Correspondent

The files may be transferred to the record sequence at the end of five years and destroyed after three years.

2

Documentation of International Comparative Statistics

"There is no difference between knowledge and temperance; for he who knows what is good and embraces it, who knows what is bad and avoids it, is learned and temperate. But they who know very well what ought to be done, and yet do quite otherwise, are ignorant and stupid."

—**Socrates**

There are three aspects of statistical sources which we need to examine: collections, use, and dissemination. Our purpose is to cover the first and last of these, leaving the use aspect to another speaker.

"The Permanent Secretary to the (U.K.) Board of Trade identified three ways in which the demand for statistics might be generated: by the policy-making part of government; form the awareness of government statisticians of gaps in available information; and by suggestions from industry that particular statistics might be collected."

This is a rather narrow approach, and certainly more applicable to a developed than a developing country. *Statistics are collected* for two main reasons: *first,* for administrative or political purposes, such as taxation, grant-making or the compilation of electoral registers; and *second* for policy-making-forecasting and monitoring economic and demographic trends. We can similarly identify two *methods of collecting statistical data* on a national basis. *First,* what might be termed "counting as they pass by": counting things or people in certain well-defined categories as they pass through some process or physical location.

For example, goods being imported or exported counted at the port (international trade statistics), people counted at an international border post (migration or tourist statistics), birth and death registration, and even some quite specialised data such as water consumption in a large city may be collected in this way. The *second* method is enumeration: a census or survey, usually with a questionnaire to be filled in, giving a snapshot of the situation at one time.

Obvious examples are population censuses, surveys of housing facilities, consumer expenditure and industrial investment intentions. A third method of data collection could be mentioned: accident. This occurs when data collected for one purpose yields additional information either within itself, or, where the data has been carefully classified, by comparison with other sources: data collected for income tax purposes will yield partial data on income distribution.

Usually, several of these methods will be needed to produce any comprehensive picture: the introductory notes to the Special Report on International Migration in the 1977 *Demographic Yearbook* indicated that data had bene acquired by a combination of border collection, registration and field surveys, and a detailed table was given as to which method or methods were used in each country covered. We shall return to the question of data collection in more detail later, but next let us look briefly at the *use to which statistics are put,* since to large degree the use governs the content and the method of collection of data.

Why do we want statistical information? Pyatt and Roe, in the introduction to their book *Social Accounting for Development Planing* (a study prepared for the International Labour Office under its World Employment Programme) said:

> "... we see statistics as an input into informed opinion and as a means of making better policy decisions. The case for statistics as a purely descriptive historical record is an extremely limited one."

There are at least four interrelated reasons for collecting statistics:

1. to monitor current events;
2. to improve economic policy-making;
3. to facilitate and make more accurate the forecasting of changes in economic variables; and
4. to enable us to understand better the relationships between various sectors of the economy.

It is apt to quote Pyatt and Roe once again.

> "... the complete (albeit relatively crude) picture which emerges generates psychological novelty by virtue of showing (Here, as elsewhere in this paper, we should remember that demographic and social data are also important in economic policy-making, so these aspects of data should also be included in our examination. They are frequently much more sensitive and difficult to obtain accurately than economic data).

Thus, before we look in detail at the dissemination of statistics by international organisations there is one aspect of the *publication* of data which is worth noting: publication means making public, and this gives a political dimension to some data publication. Statistics may show results contrary to a declared policy, and there may be a great temptation for a government to suppress or modify the data it publishes.

> Two examples, anonymous for obvious reasons, will suffice: a team of economists retained by an international organisation to prepare a report on a Middle East country, asked for the unemployment figures. "We have no unemployment," they were told "the President has a policy of full employment." One can compare the data for the number of Americans migrating to certain centrally planned economies, given by the U.S. and by the receiving country, and see the discrepancies.

No doubt, some returns may not be forthcoming for strategic reasons: for example, the U.N. *Statistical Yearbook* does not include any data for uranium production in Argentina, Austria, Brazil, Finland, India or Italy, although all these countries have substantial resources of both uranium and statisticians.

Publication, in printed form is the main method used by international organisations to disseminate the data they collect: but how do they collect it? These data are of *three types: first,* the result of a direct survey conducted by the staff of the international organisation, or by experts employed by them, and perhaps under their supervision; *second,* the result of a special survey, done at the request of the international organisation, by local national statisticians and/or subject experts; *third,* a compilation of data collected by the national statistical service to meet its own needs.

Another type, probably a subdivision of this last one, might be identified: a report produced by the international organisation's staff (or subcontracted experts) based on a variety of data sources. Of course, this delineation of types of data sources is somewhat artificial, since most published series form international organisations will comprise some, or all, of these types: one country's normally-collected series will be another's special survey; this is an aspect of international organisations' data collection we shall return to later.

For example, a not untypical section of the introductory notes to a statistical compendium reads:

> "For the preparation of this volume information was collected from all readily available sources: national and international publications, country replies to the annual questionnaires sent out by the Directorate ..., the Growth questionnaire sent out by Working Party No. 2...., miscellaneous reports and direct information provided to the O.E.C.D."

Or, from another international organisation:

> "The statistics presented in the *Demographic Yearbook* are official data unless otherwise indicated. The primary source of data for the *Yearbook* is a set of questionnaires sent annually and monthly to more than 220 national statistical services and other appropriate government offices. Data forwarded on these questionnaires are supplemented, to the extent possible, by correspondence with the national statistical services."

Now the question aries what can international organisations' statistics sources provide which is not available in a *collection of separate national statistics publications?*

The *first* answer is implied in the question: there are very few collections of statistics publications from national sources, available to the public, which could provide anything like the coverage of the international organisation's output.

Second, the international organisation, with its political muscle backing its technical expertise can elicit information from government statistical services which the latter does not normally publish itself.

Third, many government simply do not have the manpower or the expertise to collect certain data, however desirable they may be—the international organisation can provide advice, assistance, and in some cases financial support, for the carrying out of the special surveys, or training local staff to do them.

Fourth, an international organisation can put pressure on a national statistical service to provide data to a time schedule. This may be an advantage, in speeding up the publication of some nations' data, or a disadvantage in delaying the publication of another's.

Fifth, international organisations provide unbiased evaluation of (and in some cases, comment on) nationally-produced data. But it is probably the *sixth* feature of international statistical compendia which is widely regarded as the most valuable: international comparability.

Those of us who use international statistical data are aware of the great debt we owe to the statistical offices of international bodies for the work they have carried out in persuading, cajoling (perhaps even forcing?) national statistical systems to adopt standard definitions of products and industries. It is an immense task and will take many years, but the value of the results is equally immense. Sometimes they admit defeat, even in a subject one would have thought relatively straightforward, such as the land surface: "Lack of international comparability between surface area estimates arise primarily from differences in definition." (the difference in treatment of inlets, costal systems, rivers and inland lakes).

Let us now look at the three (perhaps four) *types of data collected by international organisations* and see how they match up to the possible advantages and disadvantages noted.

First, the survey: in an extreme form this would entail the organisation sending staff (either its own or staff seconded for the purpose) to collect the data or to supervise its collection. This is rare, because the organisations' statistical offices are not designed for this. More likely, they will send staff to encourage, train and perhaps supervise local statisticians in setting up, and running the machinery to produce the data. The advantage of this type of data are: minimal time lag in data production absolute control over definitions and thus comparability. The training of local staff leaves the country with expertise for the future, and supervision of collection means that the international organisation can evaluate the quality of the data and, if necessary, offset known politically-biased results. The disadvantage is that the international organisations are not geared up for this type of activity, though they are deeply involved in the training aspect. And or course, there is the political element. No government likes to admit that it cannot do the job itself and has to ask the international community to do it for it.

Remarkably, a more common scenario is when the international organisation asks an existing national statistical service to carry out a specific survey, perhaps with advice or assistance from outside experts. An example of this is the request by the Conference of European Statisticians, under the auspices of the U.N.E.C.E., for standardised data on tourism, made in 1972. As adopted by O.E.C.D. this specified, in great detail, the common data to be obtained through national holiday surveys undertaken by member countries of the O.E.C.D.

Insofar as the sponsoring organisation can lay down specific detailed definitions, and the countries adhere to these, the data will be comparable. And the national statistical offices will gain the expertise to carry out such surveys again. The price paid, however, is a time lag if the data is not already collected, and, in increasing the demands made on the national statistical service the survey may bias the priorities they have for their work. This aspect is especially important in the case of countries with small and hard-pressed statistical services, and is a point we shall return to later.

The vast majority of statistical data published by international organisations is taken from reports by national statistical offices, of data they collect because they need it themselves. This is especially true of most data about developed countries, or more accurately, countries with developed statistical services. It leaves the international organisation with the problem of reconciling data from different countries, using different definitions of terms, and/or persuading the national statistical offices to adopt standard definitions. In so far as it is successful, the comparability of data is good; if it is not successful the organisation's statisticians must re-work and data supplied to approximate comparability and aggregation.

Similarly, these statistics may be reworked by the statisticians of the international organisation on a different basis: international trade by commodity, by country, by region, by type of economy, or rebasing a series of index numbers. The last group of statistical publications of international organisations are reports, based on data already collected, but collating it in a different way, and with expert commentary added. One important example of this type of publication is the regular series of *Economic Surveys* of the member countries carried out by O.E.C.D. Using data supplied by the country, together with their own estimates, O.E.C.D. economists report on the current state and short-term forecasts for each member country. Because of the quality of the report and commentary, and the high regard in which O.E.C.D. economists are held, these reports are held in great esteem by the countries concerned.

Other, regularly published examples are the Food and Agriculture Organisation's annual review, *The State of Food and Agriculture,* and its review and forecast, *Commodity Review and Outlook.*

In the category too we must include those monographic reports containing data but not necessarily continued as a serial: again the F.A.O. produced may of these in the past, for example *The World Rice Economy in Figures* with its detailed historical data, and the *Pulp and Paper Development in Africa and the Near East,* a conference report. Considerable rationalisation of the publication of statistics has taken place in recent years. The F.A.O.'s thin *Commodity Reviews* such as *The Coconut Situation* have given way to statistical compendia like the *Production Yearbook,* a welcome change.

So far we have been talking as if publication were the only form of statistical data dissemination by international organisations: but we need to look briefly at the rising star—databanks. In the postwar period, and especially in the last ten years we have seen very great increases in the quantity of data collected, the specificity of that data, the demand for data by non-government bodies and above all, the inevitable use of computers to process the ever-increasing volume of statistical returns. International organisations' statistical offices are subject to these pressures no less than the national statisticians who supply them, and although the national offices national statisticians who supply them, and although the national offices have generally speaking been more advanced in the use of computers, the international statistical agencies have produced some valuable databanks. The most obvious use has bene in the processing of data and the mechanisation of the typesetting of printed tables: many European Community statistical publications are produced in this way. But this is merely the mechanics of printing, although the use of computers to produce microfiche editions of statistical serials has speeded up their publication: O.E.C.D. and the S.O.E.C. have both adopted this means of rapid publication of international trade data.

Much more important aspects are that large quantities of data can be obtained now on magnetic tape, ready for use in the customer's own computer, that some of the very specialised data which it would be uneconomic to publish in conventional ways can be made available to meet customers' specific needs, and that those statistical offices which have matching software such as macroeconomic models, may be persuaded to make them publicly available, enabling non-official bodies to use the forecasting models *and* data used by governments. The final advantages of databanks are that they can be constantly updated, with new estimates replacing earlier ones, and they are cheap to produce.

All advances carry with the *drawbacks. First,* the problem of access: statisticians are notoriously bad at providing adequate indexes to their published tables, and the same criticism applies to databanks. *Second,* when an individual user extracts a data series he does not automatically, or even easily, obtain the "small print" — the details of the method of collection, and the definitions used — which is so vital for the proper appreciation of the data. The *third* problem relates to developing countries: the statistical offices of small or developing countries are under extreme pressure to collect and process data, and have great difficulty in training statisticians of the high quality needed for this work. Computerisation adds another, technological, dimension to their problem. One might refer to this as the problem of "appropriate technology" (a term beloved by development economists) applied to statistical work. One aspect of the computerisation of data does not yet seem to have been appreciated: vast quantities of very detailed data are being printed conventionally when the demand for the data is very limited. Might it not be more economic to supply this in a cheaper format only to those bodies particularly interested? The Statistical Office of the European Communities is a particular offender in this context, with extremely detailed published data on, the example, the weekly prices of specific agricultural produce in certain towns throughout the Community.

All in all, then, we must accept that the development of databanks as a means of data dissemination will continue, but that it raises problems for all users of data, and for some collectors as well.

Finally, we will to consider two very fundamental questions about international statistics: is the international organisations' involvement in statistical publication a good thing? Are the international organisations doing enough to stimulate the right and a better quality statistical output? The questions are related and I propose to treat them together.

Remember! the benefits of international organisations' statistical efforts can be catalogued:

1. they collect together data from many different sources into one convenient package;
2. they provide standard definitions and persuade national statistical offices to adapt to (if not adopt) them; and
3. they assist embryo statistical offices to develop their expertise.

The family of international organisations which we cell the United Nations, have, over the years, amounts of money and effort to improve the quantity and quality of useful data available to economists and planners throughout the world, and especially in and for developing countries. This work is very fully described in Part 1 of the United Nations Statistical Office publication *Directory of International Statistics* (New York, U.K. 1975) (Statistical Papers, Series M, No. 56).

The main forms of technical assistance provided by the United Nations in the statistical field are advisory experts, and training. This latter activity may take the form of support for training centers, courses, conferences, and workshops. In parallel, of course, has been the publication of manuals on methods, especially of sampling and census-taking, and the compilation of agreed international classification schemes for industries, products and occupations.

From Pyatt and Roe says again:

> "A very large amount of the increased postwar availability of macroeconomic data.... is due to the efforts of the United Nations and other international agencies in producing manuals explaining the sort of data which are 'needed,' the classifications which are appropriate, and the methods of collection. These same agencies have also contributed by supplying technical assistance personnel to help carry through their recommendations."

And in the similar vein from the United Nations itself, explaining the purpose of one of its statistical programmes:

> "... its basic aim is to make optimum use of all available resources to build up an effective and enduring statistical infrastructure ... with a resulting improvement of related national statistical services."

No doubt, we are all well aware of the benefits which the

international organisations' statisticians have given to the economic community. *But there is disquiet* among some of the development economists working in the field, in both developing and developed countries: "In retrospect, it can be doubted whether the efforts made by the United Nations Statistical Office and the Technical Assistance Administration in the course of the past fifteen years to improve statistics in the underdeveloped countries have led to entirely desirable consequences. For reasons of prestige, many of these nations have felt compelled to concentrate their statistical efforts on compilation of such global estimates as those of national income, capital formation and savings. When an expert, under the auspices of the UN, has gone to a country on a short term assignment, pressure has been brought upon him to help the local statisticians in assembling glamorous macroeconomic estimates. Fashion has thus pushed necessity aside. As a result, development of basic statistics such as data on production, prices, population movements, growth and distribution of labour force has been on the whole neglected."

More specifically, the critics say, *first* that the data being asked for, or at least the detail being demanded, is irrelevant for developing countries. Prof. Hans Singer in an I.L.O. document, for example: "Once it is generally realised that much of the data now collected (such as GNP growth ... on export growth ....) are irrelevant to development (the purpose of which is to reduce or eliminate poverty) it becomes clear that this sort of data collection could be discontinued in order to switch resources to obtaining more relevant data."

For example — taken at random from the 1978 United Nations *Statistical Yearbook:* steel consumption in Togo, cotton consumption in Nicaragua, sugar consumption by industry in Thailand, and the floor area of new non-residential building in Kenya. Sometimes, of course, national statisticians do not deliver the goods: palm oil production, and milk production, by animal, for most developing countries is given as estimates by the F.A.O. Data on wheat production, however, is almost complete, but a high proportion is in developed countries.

Second, the critics add that the task being set developing countries is too big:

> "... many see the SNA (System of National Accounts) as a monolithic, excessively ambitious, dogmatic structure which 'requires' developing countries to produce data in which they have no analytical interest, using classifications and conventions which are quite inappropriate to their circumstances, and so on." (Pyatt and Roe).

Third, following on from these criticisms is the fear that the demands made on local statisticians by international organisations bias the work of the local offices. Pyatt and Roe gives considerable space in their book to the statistical problems besetting economists working on Sri Lanka, despite Snodgrass' comment: "The body of economic statistics available for Ceylon must certainly rank as one of the most complete and accurate in the world for a country of such low per capita income."

Further additionally, there is the problem of reliability: despite the enormous increase in the availability of data for developing countries the statistical documentation is often poor in terms of the reliability of the data — often due to pressure of work on the local statistical offices. What reliance can be placed, for example, on the data for mattress production (sprung or filled with any material) in El Salvador? we raise this mainly because of the data themselves: 12,000 in 1968, 101,000 in 1969, back to 26,000 in 1970.

The international organisations' technical assistance is felt to be of less permanent benefit than had been anticipated.

The United Nations Secretariat notes:

"Interest by international and bilateral agencies has also tended to follow on a specific need, usually of the agency concerned, leaving behind little of the enduring nature after the survey has been completed."

So, what conclusions can we draw? Certainly the effects of various international organisations' statistical offices have produced large and valuable compilations of statistical data, on a reasonably comparable basis, which would not have otherwise been widely available. These data are probably of more value to economists, economic advisers and the organisations themselves than to the developing countries which produce so many of them. We have a sneaking feeling that these economists are reaping the benefits, and that price is being paid by the third world countries. If the statisticians in international organisations can be persuaded by development economists to trim the demands they make on the small expert resources of developing countries, to reduce the number of data they ask for, and to ensure that the detail requested is relevant to the needs of the supplying country, and not simply needed to provide blanket-coverage for the world, then some of the problems will be ameliorated.

REFERENCES

1. Graham Pyatt and Alan Roe: *Social Accounting for Development Planning, with special reference to Sri Lanka.* Cambridge: Cambridge University Press, 1977, page. 15.

2. International Labour Office: *Time of Transition:* a mid-term review of the Second United Nations Development Decade. Geneva: I.L.O., 1975, page 83.

3. Mitra, A.: Underdeveloped statistics, *Economic Development and Cultural Change.* 9.3 (Ap. 1963), part 1.

4. Organisation for Economic Cooperation and Development: *Labour Force Statistics, 1966-77.* Paris: O.E.C.D., Introduction.

5. United Nations. *Demographic Yearbook, 1977. New York: U.N. Technical notes on the statistical tables, page 17.*

6. United Nations. Secretariat. *The National Household Survey Capability Programme (NHSCP), Prospectus.* Consultative Meeting on the National Household Survey Capability Programme, 21-22 June 1979, New York. (ST/ESA/STAT 92.) New York: U.N., 1979, page. 1.

3

PROCUREMENT PROCESS

"Be unselfish. That is the first and final commandment for those who would be useful, and happy in their usefulness. If you think of yourself only, you cannot develop because you are choking the sources of development, which is spiritual expansion through thought for others."

—Dr. Charles W. Eliot

Procurement of books and other library material is an important task. Various steps and srategies are adopted for this. Herein we will describe the usually followed processes of the procurement of library materials.

Selection

The library materials include books/publications, audiovisual and nonbook materials and periodicals. In this chapter, procurement of books/publications has been dealt with. The process of book selection is very important as judicious judgement has to be exercised in selecting books, current as well as retrospective, conforming to the acquisition policy of the library. While selecting books the needs and demands of the readers, budget provision and specific and related subjects of the library are to be borne in mind.

Sources

Normally the books are selected from the following sources:

1. Books received on approval from the suppliers.
2. Books selection tools.
3. Reviews in newspapers and journals.
4. Catalogues of publishers and booksellers.
5. Bibliographies.
6. Lists of new additions of various libraries.
7. Suggestions of the readers.
8. Book Exhibitions and Book Fairs. (In India every two years, a World Book Fair is held. The Fair for selecting good books.)

Tools

A comprehensive list of Book Selection tools is given at the end of this chapter the following tools, however, are used regularly.

A. Indian Tools

1. Publishing in India
2. Indian National Bibliography
3. Accession list, South Asia
4. Indian Books in Print
5. Catalogues of Publishers.

B. British Tools

1. Bookseller
2. British Book News
3. British Books in Print

4. British National Bibliography
5. Times Literary Supplement.

C. American Tools

1. American Book Publishing Record
2. American Bookseller
3. Books in Print
4. Book List
5. Book Review Digest
6. Choice
7. New York Times Book Review.
8. Publishers Weekly.

Steps Involved

1. Opinion about the new books selected from the various sources should be sought from officers/readers/ teachers and users according to their subject of specialisation. *(A specimen of the note is appended at Appendix 3-11).*
2. The list of books suggested and selected is prepared and sent to the Book-Selection Committee/Library Committee Library Authority along with relevant recommendations for final approval.
3. Book Selection cards are prepared, giving all possible bibliographical information for the books finally selected. Duplication of books selected is to be checked against the following sources:
   - Library catalogue
   - Books on approval
   - Books on order

- Books selected
- Books in process

After checking for duplicates, the cards are filed b the Books selection sequence. The specimen of book selection card is given below:

4. Book selection cards for books which are neither in the library nor on order or in process are passed on to the Acquisition Section. Cards for books which are either in library catalogue or on order or in process are withdrawn from the main Book-selection sequence and kept separately.

Role of the Staff

The role of the staff engaged in Book-selection process is very important. Such a staff should be familiar with:

- Collection of the library and its policy.
- Book-selection tools.
- Readers and their needs.
- Book trade.
- Publishers and Booksellers and their subjects of specialisation.
- Newspaper and journals which review books.
- Advertisements and Announcements of pre-publication prices of books.
- Constant perusal and reading of journals, newspapers, catalogues and bibliographies is essential.

Acquisition

The acquisition of books/publications is a fundamental function which lays the foundation of library service. Library book acquisition is the library activity through which it obtains the possession of library books and other reading materials so as to provide the reader with the information he or she wants when he or she wants it. It is therefore important to formulate an acquisition policy in a library, which of course will vary from library to library. The reading material is acquired in a library through purchase, gift and exchange according to its policy.

How to Purchase

Librarians may consult Government of India decision for purchase of books etc. in Rules 99 and 116 of the *General Financial Rules*, 1963 (Third Edition) wherein they have stated that the position of library books, etc. is different from that of other stores. This has saved the librarians of the ordeal of calling quotations for purchase of books. Inter alia procedures for write-off, disposal of mutilated/damaged books and physical verification of books, have also been laid down in these rules.

The books are purchased by placing orders with the booksellers for the books required and selected from various sources.

Following office note is written for soliciting the approval of the competent authority for the books to be purchased:

> Books *listed in the enclosed list/books listed below have been recommended [or purchase by various officers/renders mentioned against each.*
>
> *Chairman/Director/Chief Librarian may kindly see for approval*

After the approval is available a letter is sent to one of the approved booksellers.

The cards of books approved for purchase out of the books selected from various sources and bibliographical tools, are prepared and kept in the sequence of 'Books on Order.'

Librarian may keep a check on the supply of books ordered, the receipt of bills of selected books and in case of their non-receipt the suppliers may be reminded.

Books Received on Approval

Books are also purchased directly from the books received on approval. Books received on approval are placed before the 'Books Selection Committee' or the 'Library Committee,' if there is such a committee for selection. An office note for such selected books may be sent to the competent authority before those are purchased, in the following manner:

> Books *mentioned below/books listed in the enclosed list have been selected for purchase by the 'Books Selection Committee' or the 'Library Committee' out of the books received on approval.*
>
> *Before these are purchased, Chairman/Director/ Chief Librarian/ . . . may kindly see.*

As soon as the note is signed, letters may be sent to respective booksellers from whom the books were received, for sending the pre-receipted bills in triplicate for necessary payment.

After the orders of the books selected for purchase, out of the books received on approval, have been placed, the cards for these books are prepared and filed under the "Books Purchased" sequence. If the cards of these books are available in the "Books on Order" sequence, the same are removed from there and their orders are cancelled with the respective booksellers.

Approval of Booksellers

It is essential to draw up a list of booksellers to be approved for the supply of books during the whole financial year. Every year before the commencement of the financial year it is necessary to fix up terms and conditions for the supply of books both Indian and foreign. The booksellers whose services in the past year had not been found satisfactory may be dropped from the list of suppliers. After the quotations are received and approved, the standard conversion rates may be established for transaction during the whole financial year. In India the rates, terms and conditions fixed by the Good Offices Committee from time to time are almost followed by all the libraries. To ensure prompt supply of books and for efficient service the library may fix up its own additional terms and conditions for the suppliers. Librarians are required to ensure that the decision for purchase of books received on approval is taken within 30 days from the date of their receipt Payment of bills, when received, should be paid within 60 days. Delayed decision for purchase and payment of bills discourages booksellers in doing business with libraries. All the books received from the suppliers will be checked thoroughly so that the books found damaged may not be stamped, accessioned and are returned to the suppliers promptly. The ownership stamp may be affixed at three places in the books (i) on the back of the title page; (ii) at the bottom of the confidential page decided upon by the Library; and (iii) at the last page of the book. Thereafter the books will be entered in the Accession Register.

The accession numbers shall also be placed on all the three copies of the bill when received against respective books and also on the order cards. The books when stamped and accessioned are sent to the Processing Section along with their respective cards taken out from the 'Books Purchased' sequence. Such cards are then filed in the 'Books in Process' sequence. There are instances when a book is found to be defective after some time of its purchase. In such cases the supplier should be asked to replace the book. While returning the book the library stamp affixed should be cancelled.

Payment of Bills

Payment of bills is also a major task. When the bills are received, the library should enter their particulars in the bill register and verify the titles of the books with the letters sent to the suppliers. The library will also check the price of each book mentioned in the bill with the price printed on it If it is not printed then it may be checked in other reference tools. However, it is the sole responsibility of the bookseller to satisfy the library about the cost of the book either by showing the invoice from where they have received the book or by showing the catalogue received from the distributor or publisher. The total in the bill, exchange rate charged for the books priced in foreign currency, may also be checked, before passing the bills.

The bills should bear the following certificate by the booksellers on them:

> Certified *that books supplied are not remainder stock and are latest editions. Further certified that prices charged are correct and those* fixed *by the publishers.*

The bills, not found in order, may be returned to the supplier with necessary instructions for correcting them. Affix the following rubber stamp on each copy of the bill:

> The books have been received in good condition and have been entered in the Accession Register. The Accession Numbers are indicated against each item. Certified that no previous payment has been made in respect of this bill. The bill is in order and may be passed for payment of Rs (Rupees)

The bills after they have been endorsed properly and signed by the librarian are sent to the Cash/Accounts Section after making entries in the "Bills Forwarding Register" for making necessary payment to the suppliers. In come government departments the sanction order is necessary. A close watch on the expenditure for purchase of books has to be kept so that it does not exceed the allotted budget.

Some publishers advertise pre-publication prices, which are much less than the published prices. Library staff should keep track of such announcements and make use of such offers while purchasing books.

Gratis/Gift

Books received as gratis are Government publications by and large. In 1950s the Ministries and Departments used to send the copies of their publications free of cost to other Ministries and Departments. As the time passed by, the Ministries/Departments started sending their publications to select Ministries/Departments. Now when the cost of printing and paper has gone up most of the Ministries/Departments have priced their publications.

Even then if they receive requests for complimentary copies from Government Departments they do entertain such requests and send copies of their publications as gratis. Librarians are, therefore, advised not to lose the opportunity of getting such publications on complimentary basis. Besides, there are publications of research institutes and autonomous bodies which can also be obtained as gratis. In cases where efforts fail to get the complimentary copies of the publications, method of purchase is to be used. If the library or its Department/Organisation is bringing out a journal, the librarian .should write to the publishers to send their books as complimentary review copies, for review in the journal.

Exchange

Publications on exchange basis can be obtained only by those libraries whose Ministries/Departments are bringing out their own publications and journals.

As soon as the books/publications are received on complimentary /exchange basis, those are accessioned and sent to Processing Section for further action. Processing cards for these publications are invariably prepared.

Good Offices Committee

The Good Offices Committee (GOC), a voluntary organisation, was formed in 1972. It was established with the aim of streamlining the procedures of book trade and to follow the uniform terms of book supplies to libraries and also to ensure a fair working margin to booksellers and an efficient service to the libraries. To begin with, the GOC was constituted of representatives of Government of India Librarians Associations (GILA), Indian Library Association (ILA), Delhi State Booksellers' and Publishers' Association (DSBPA). Federation of Publishers' and Booksellers' Association in India (FPBA), Delhi University, University Grants Commission and Ministry of Human Resource Development (as observers).

Later on a few more were included. The Committee used to meet after every two months and, after taking into consideration the fluctuations in the currency rates, decided on the rate of conversion for the sale of books and periodicals.

Remarkably, the following main guidelines were formulated:

(i) In order to bring about a uniformity of GOC recommended conversion rates, library discount and standardisation in the terms of supply, the Librarians are advised to follow its recommendations and deal with the members of Book Trade Associations.

(ii) Books on approval should be finalised/returned within 30 days. The payment for the books approved should be made within 60 days of the receipt of the bills. The bill is to be raised by the supplier at the conversion rate prevailing on the date when the books are finally selected for purchase in the library.

(iii) The suppliers shall certify on the bills that only the latest editions have been supplied and they are not remainder titles.

As of now the discount on books varies from one library to another. With mushroom growth of educational institutions discount has become a major concern for suppliers in the present competitive age. However, generally uniform discount of 10 per cent was fixed for English books (both Indian and foreign). For Short Discount and No-Discount books a formula was devised so that the bookseller gets a margin of 15 per cent.

Questions have been raised from time to time about validity of GOC rules due to many factors. W.e.f. 23-3-92 discount on Indian publications was increased to 15 per cent and w.e.f. 1.9.94 the markup of 5 per cent on foreign currency was abolished.

The present discount rates as decided by GOC are as follows:

Discount

1. Foreign Publications

All books of foreign origin (with the exception of the following special categories) are subject to a uniform discount of 10 per cent of the published price converted into Indian Rupees:

Special Categories

Short/no discount tides or titles procured from abroad against specific orders.

The importer or the library supplier is expected to work on a margin of 15 per cent. The invoice is to be prepared on the following terms:

Published price minus (—) discount earned plus (+) handling charges of the overseas agent, if any. Handling charges will include freight, clearance, bank and postal charges. Documentary evidence to be submitted by the supplier to the library on demand. The discount on remainder titles will be 30 per cent of the published price and should be charged through separate invoices.

Indian Publications

(a) Central and State Government publications — No discount.

(b) Paper cover editions, books in regional languages, textbooks and short discount reference books will be subject to 10 per cent discount.

(c) Other Indian publications in English will be subject to 15 per cent discount.

Journals

Discount : No discount

Short Discount and No Discount Journals

The agent will apply the same formula as in the case of books.

All subscriptions shall be recorded at the conversion rate as approved by the Good Offices Committee.

The subscription agent will charge publishers' current subscription rate and postage as indicated in the publishers' catalogues. Wherever concessional rates are available, the agent will charge accordingly.

The conversion rate charged in proforma invoice for advance payment by the agent will be valid for a period of 60 days. Against payment received after this period, the agent will raise supplementary bill/credit note for any revision in conversion rate as applied in the proforma invoice and as applicable on the date of receipt of payment.

The subscriber shall pay in advance full amount of subscription in Indian currency at the rate of conversion fixed by the GOC prevailing on the date of invoicing. Any subsequent change in the rate of subscription/postage conversion shall be claimed by the agent through supplementary invoice. However, in case of any subsequent reduction in the rate of subscription/postage, credit notes will be drawn at the same rates as charged in the invoices. For supplying journals to the subscriber imported by the agent by air freight, the agent will charge a levy at 7.5 per cent of the total subscription rate. However, the agent will not levy any additional surcharges where the publishers supply journals to India at subscription rate inclusive of air surcharge.

The recommendations of GOC should be respected by all the Librarians, Booksellers, Publishers and Distributors, in the interest of healthy book trade in India. GOC is a voluntary organisation, without any statutory power and the librarians and book-trade people should work together with mutual trust and cooperation. Librarians should not always dictate their terms and should take into consideration the difficulties encountered by booksellers in providing prompt service to librarians in the delivery of ordered books. Wholesellers and distributors should increase their trade discount to retail booksellers so that they are compensated for higher discount which they are forced to offer to libraries. A circular comprising exchange rates, terms and conditions, is issued immediately after the meeting of GOC is held. A copy of the circular in made available by the Delhi State Booksellers' and Publishers Association and other bodies.

Important Steps

1. The Book Selection Tools shall be received and examined regularly.
2. Cards shall be prepared for the books selected.
3. Duplication shall be checked with library catalogue and sequences of Books on Approval, Books on Order and Books in Process.
4. Cards related to selected books shall be passed on, to acquisition section.
5. Action may be initiated before the commencement of financial year for fixing the terms of supply of Indian as well as foreign publications and also preparing the list of approved booksellers for the ensuing year.
6. All approval memos of the books received on approval shall be filed separately for each vendor in chronological order.
7. The books received on approval but rejected and returned to the booksellers shall be struck off from the approval memo and the signature of the person acknowledging receipt shall be obtained on the approval memo itself with date.
8. The price charged for each book by the bookseller shall be checked with the price printed on the book or from the publishers' catalogue if not printed on the book.
9. In case, price charged by the bookseller is questionable, he should be asked to present the invoice in original and the Librarian should certify that the invoice has been examined and the price charged by the bookseller

is found to be correct. For books which are rare and out of print, the prices are negotiated.

10. The booksellers should be instructed to submit their bills for each order and certify on the bill that only the published prices have been charged. The bills should be submitted by the booksellers in triplicate.
11. Each bill shall be stamped as mentioned and passed for payment. Triplicate copy of each bill accepted and passed for payment shall be filed chronologically in the library file.

LIST OF BOOK-SELECTION TOOLS

Australia

Australian Book Review. Monthly. Australia.

Canada

Canadian Books in Print. Annual. Toronto, Toronto University Press, 1967.

France

1. International Book Year Newsletter. Monthly. Paris, UNESCO, International Book Year Unit, 1971.
2. International Association of Literary Critics' Bulletin. Semi-Annual. Paris, International Association of Literary Critics.

Hungary

Hungarian Book Review. Quarterly. Budapest, Kulture, 1959.

India

1. Accession List, South Asia (Afghanistan, Bangladesh, Bhutan, India, Maldives, Nepal, Pakistan and Sri

Lanka). Monthly. New Delhi, U.S. Library of Congress Office. (Formerly Accession List of India). 1962.

2. Ajanta Book News. Delhi, Ajanta Books International.
3. Asian Books Newsletter. Monthly. Calcutta. 1966 –
4. ASR Newsletter. Quarterly. Melkote. Academy of Sanskrit Research.
5. ATC News. Monthly. Bangalore, Asian Trading Corporation.
6. BBPA News. Quarterly. Bombay, Bombay Booksellers and Publishers' Association.
7. Bibliography of English Publications on India. Annual. Delhi, D.K.F Trust 1976-78.
8. Book Centre. Monthly. Delhi, Hind Pustak Bhandar.
9. Book News. Monthly. New Delhi, Allied Publishers.
10. The Civil and Military Review. Monthly. New Delhi, Deep & Deep Publications.
11. CSIR News. Monthly. New Delhi, Publications and Information Directorate, 1992 –
12. GIRH and FWT. Monthly. Ambathurai, The Gandhigram Institute of Rural Health and Welfare Trust.
13. GSP News. Monthly. Anand, Gujarat Sahitya Prakash.
14. Higginbothams News. Monthly. Madras, Higginbothams Ltd.
15. IIPA Newsletter. Monthly. New Delhi, Indian Institute of Public Administration.
16. Indian Book Industry. Monthly. New Delhi, Sterling Publishers, 1969 –
17. Indian Books in Print. Sher Singh (Ed.) 3 vols. Delhi, Indian Bibliographies Bureau, 1981 –

18. Indian National Bibliography. Quarterly upto 1963 and monthly from 1964 and annual cumulations. Calcutta, Central Reference Library, 1957 –
19. JNU News. Monthly. New Delhi, Jawaharlal Nehru University.
20. JBA. Monthly. New Delhi. Jain Book Agency.
21. List of Books — New Arrivals. Quarterly. Delhi, Shipra Library Services, 1988 –
22. MLBD News. Monthly. Delhi, Motilal Banarasidas.
23. NBT Newsletter. Monthly. New Delhi, National Book Trust.
24. Prakashan Samachar. Monthly. Delhi, Rajkamal Prakashan, 1953.
25. Publishers Monthly. New Delhi, S. Chand and Co., 1959 –
26. Publishing in India; a Journal of Book Trade and Industry. Monthly. New Delhi, D.K. Publishers' Distributors.
27. Recent Indian Books; a quarterly catalogue of Indian Publications. Quarterly. New Delhi, Federation of Publishers and Booksellers' Associations in India, 1975 –
28. Rupa Book News. Monthly. New Delhi. Rupa and Co.
29. Sahitya Akademi. Quarterly. New Delhi, Sahitya Akademi.
30. Upper and Lower Sardar Patel Institute of Economic and Social Research Quarterly. Ahmedabad, Sardar Patel Institute of Economic and Social Research.

31. SAT News. Quarterly. Patancheru, International Crops Research Institute for Semi-Arid Tropics.
32. Shri Ram Centre Review. Biennial. New Delhi, Shri Ram Centre for Industrial Relations and Human Resources.
33. Sterling Book Fare. Monthly. New Delhi, Sterling Publishers.
34. Vikas News. Monthly. New Delhi, Vikas Publishing House, 1974 –
35. Upper and Lower Update: Bhavan's Books. Bombay, Bharatiya Vidya Bhavan.

Italy

Italian Books in Print. London, Bowker-Saur.

Japan

Japan Book News. Monthly. Tokyo, Publishing Research Associates. 1970 –

New Zealand

New Zealand Book World. Journal of the New Zealand Book Trade. Six issues per year. New Zealand, John Paul Production, 1973 –

Pakistan

Bookseller. Monthly. Lahore, Pakistan Publishers and Booksellers, 1964 –

Rumania

Romanian Books. Quarterly. Bucharest, Foreign Relations Department Publishing Centre, 1964 –

Russia

Russian Books in Print Plus. London, Bowker-Saur, 1989–

U.K.

1. ASLIB Booklist. Monthly. London. Aslib. 1935.
2. Bookseller, the organ of the book trade. Weekly. London. J. Whitakers and Sons, 1958 –
3. British Books News. Monthly. London, British Council 1940.
4. British Books in Print. Annual (2 vols.). London, J. Whitakers and Sons, 1967 –
5. British National Bibliography, Weekly plus two Inter cumulations and annual Vol. London, British Library, Bibliographical Services Division, 1950 –
6. HMSO Monthly Catalogue of Publications. London. HMSO Office.
7. Paperbacks in Print. Annual. London, J. Whitakers and Sons, 1965 –
8. Times Education Supplement. Weekly. London. Times Newspapers Ltd., 1910 –
9. Times Higher Education Supplement. Weekly. London. Times Newspapers Ltd., 1971 –
10. Times Literary Supplement. Weekly. London, Times Newspapers Ltd., 1902 –
11. Whitaker's Books of the Month and Books to come. Monthly. London, J. Whitakers and Sons. 1970 –
12. Whitaker's Cumulative Book List Quarterly London, J. Whitakers and Sons, 1924 –

U.S.A.

1. American Book Publishing Record. Monthly with annual and five-year cumulations. New York, RR. Bowker and Co., 1961 –

2. American Bookseller. Monthly. New York, Booksellers Publishing Inc.
3. Rooks in Print. Annual. New York, R.R. Bowker and Co., 1948 –
4. Books in Print Supplement. Annual. New York, R.R. Bowker, 1973 –
5. Booklist. Semi-Monthly. Chicago, American Library Association, 1905 –
6. Book Review Digest; an index to reviews of current books. Monthly (except Feb. and July). New York, H.W. Wilson and Co., 1905 –
7. Choice, Monthly (except bi-monthly in July and Aug.) Middletown, Association of College and Research Libraries, a division of the American Library Association, 1964 –
8. Cumulative Book. Index. Monthly with three months and annual cumulations. New York, H.W. Wilson, 1898 –
9. Monthly Catalogue of US Government Publications. Monthly. Washington D.C., Government Printing Press, 1910 –
10 National Union Catalogue. Nine monthly issues and three quarterly cumulations. Washington D.C., Library of Congress, 1956 –
11. New York Review of Books 22 issues in a year. New York, Nyrev Inc., 1963 –
12. New York Times Book Review. Weekly. New York, New York Times Co., 1896 –
13. Paper bound books in Print Biannual. New York, R.R. Bowker and Co., 1955 –

14. Publishers Trade List Annual. New York, R.R. Bowker & Co.
15. Publishers Weekly. Weekly. New York, RR Bowker and Co., 1872 –
16. Subject Guide to Books in Print Annual. New York, R.R Bowker and Co., 1957 –
17. Subject Guide to Forthcoming Books. Bimonthly. New York, RR Bowker and Co., 1967 –

Other Countries

1. Asian Book Development Quarterly. Tokyo, Asian Culture Centre for Japan (formerly Tokyo Book Development Centre Newsletter), 1969 –
2. Best Sellers. Monthly. Philadelphia, North American Publishing Company, 1946 –
3. Book Talk. 5 issues in a year. Albuquerque, New Measure Book League, 1970 –
4. Books at Iowa Semi-annual. Iowa City, Friends of the University of Iowa Libraries, University of Iowa, 1964 –
5. International Books in Print. New York, K.G. Saur Munchen, 1979 –
6. Overseas Books. Monthly. London, Publishing and Distributing Co., 1971 –
7. South Asian Book News. Monthly. Durham, Duke University, 1968 –
8. U.S. Library of Congress. Accession List Brazil. Bimonthly. Washington, U.S. Library of Congress, Overseas Operation Division.
9. U.S. Library of Congress. Accession List Eastern Africa.

Bimonthly. Washington, U.S. Library of Congress, Overseas Operation Division, 1968 –

10. U.S. Library of Congress. Accession List. Middle East Bimonthly. Washington, U.S. Library of Congress, Overseas Operation Division. 1968 –
11. U.S. Library of Congress. Accession List. South Asia. Monthly. Washington, U.S. Library of Congress, Overseas Operation Division, 1981 –
12. U.S. Library of Congress. Accession List. South East Asia. Monthly. Washington, U.S. Library of Congress, Overseas Operation Division. 1975 –

    (Supersedes: U.S. Library of Congress Accession List. Indonesia, Malaysia, Singapore and Brunnei).

Now some of the tools listed above have defunet and many new bulletins etc. are being published by different organisations or individual publishers. Most publishers— Indian and foreign have their websites. Google, Yahoo and other search engines provide vital information on books, journals etc. Online bookstores also provide information about books. Modern day libraries avail these services widely.

4

GUIDELINES FOR SOFTWARE AND SYSTEM SELECTION

"Whoever fears to submit any question to the test of free discussion, loves his own opinion than the truth."

—Ancient Proverb

In fact, the present era of information and communication technology (ICT) places several options in the library planner's hands. Selecting a microcomputer system is a complex and challenging process. The continual changes and new offerings in hardware and software add to the difficulties, but a methodical approach in determining what the system is intended to do and what available systems can meet these requirements will make the process easier. The initial decision in selecting a microcomputer system is to determine exactly what the system is meant to support: acquisitions, circulations, online files, word processing, a combination of these or various other options. The micro configuration will be determined by the kind of work it is expected to perform.

The library must also decide whether to purchase packaged software or to develop its own. Many library applications programmes exist, but few are being marketed. A major problem in purchasing or sharing existing programmes is the incompatibility of various microcomputers and of applications programmes written on them, although recent developments promise to resolve some incompatibilities. Another option is simply to purchase a micro and experiment; several libraries have chosen this alternative. However, the decision in this case is to purchase a learning experience rather than an application. The library may well discover that its micro is not the best machine for a given application or that desirable software is incompatible with it.

It is apt to note that the library must also evaluate the capabilities of different systems and analyse costs, including those for staff, site and data transfer, as well as for actual purchase and maintenance of hardware and software. In addition, the library must select a vendour and, in many cases, should prepare a contract. Whether to hire a consultant and whether the library is required to request bids for a system are other questions.

Here we discuss these issues, all of which must be addressed in selecting a microcomputer system.

Remember, automating any function should begin with a needs assessment. Such a review requires a difficult and time-consuming analysis of current procedures to determine why each action is necessary. It is often hard to be objective since the staff is likely to see established procedures as familiar and comfortable as well as functional. However, a major purpose of automation is to improve existing procedures or services.

Can any steps be eliminated or combined. Will tasks be less time-consuming? The assessment should result in a current statement of the library's functions and requirements and an awareness of the opportunities that a computer offers. From a management perspective, the bottom line is money: Will use of a micro-computer result in higher or lower operational costs for the library's service's? In determining the fiscal impact of automation, many variables must be considered. A word processing package may reduce the typing time needed to prepare user manuals or library guides. Online preparation of acquisition order forms may eliminate the need for an order card file. A computer index record with multiple access points can replace multiple catalog cards or various entries in a printed index.

Staff reaction to technology is a major determinant of the success of automation. Although there is often resistance to change, especially change that introduces new technology, a computer system can actually improve job satisfaction. Once staff members gain a basic understanding of the computer, they frequently develop a sense of achievement at having mastered it and having moved into the new era of technology.

This can result in such observable improvements as better morale and subsequent increases in productivity. In contrast, if staff members fear that a machine may eliminate jobs, they will consciously or subconsciously fight against the changes introduced. It is important that staff realise the advantages of automation—how the computer will assist their work and allow them to be involved in other more challenging responsibilities. However, automation is frequently intended to reduce the number of employees required to provide the existing services of the library. Increased productivity or the elimination of many repetitious tasks may reduce staffing needs and provide some very apparent cost savings.

To avoid major staff resistance and lowered morale that can impede productivity, the library must make it clear why cuts are needed. In the case of budget restrictions, the computer becomes a tool to alleviate some of the problems of the reduced staff. Many times, the microcomputer assumes tasks that are clerical and time-consuming and that are often handled by temporary or part-time help, for example, student assistants in educational settings. Since the turnover in such jobs is usually high, the overall impact on morale may be minimised.

It is remarkable, that the most difficult area of cost justification in libraries seems to be embodied in the phrase "improved services." Determining the cost benefit of improved services is difficult but not impossible. A microcomputer may make a new service possible at a far lower additional cost than would be required to provide the service manually. For example, lists of new titles may be generated as a by-product of an acquisitions system, yet no additional compilation and typing are required. Improved access to information, such as keyword search capabilities to augment the traditional subject term approach, is more difficult to justify.

However, the cost of generating a record, regardless of the types of access points, is high; if greater use of the data base is possible, then the cost of creating the file is better justified. If the accessibility of the information is doubled, the investment in the collection and in the system can be viewed as more cost-effective. If a public library's services are used by local businesses, one can even argue that their incomes and impact on the community are being supported by the system. An evaluation of current procedures may also reveal that a microcomputer system can reduce the library's operational costs. This may take various forms, including eliminating the need for equipment with expensive lease and maintenance costs such as keypunch machines or minicomputers.

A micro may take up less space than existing equipment, or it may replace manual operations that consumed large work areas. Floor space is expensive, and automation may make room for additional staff or operations. Supplies for micro-computers may be more or less expensive than those used in current operations; the library must look carefully at this aspect since it is a continual cost rather than part of the initial investment.

Upgradation

The decision to automate can take three directions: purchase existing software that meets the library's requirements; purchase software that can be modified or develop the programmes in-house. To determine the best alternative, the library should evaluate existing software to determine what is available and to what extent it can meet the library's needs. For many straightforward or single-function applications, existing software packages may provide the easiest and most economical answer.

Suitable Software

If the library has some in-house expertise with programming microcomputers, the option of modifying existing application packages should be considered. Software that has been developed for library support, but does not quite handle all the desired functions, may be expandable.

Careful analysis should reveal whether some aspects of the design logic in the existing software could prevent the desired enhancements. In many cases, however, it will be more cost-effective to upgrade an existing package than to start from the beginning. While expanding library packages may be feasible, modifying standard business packages is less likely to succeed. Libraries have attempted to modify inventory control systems for bibliographic control on mainframes and minicomputers with limited success; it is not likely that micros would have any greater success.

The major problems in converting business systems are the file structures and the record formats. Bibliographic records require multiple access points or indexes to the record; most inventory or business accounting systems have only one or two. Bibliographic records are also extremely complex; they have variable-length fields of information as well as variable occurrences of fields.

For example, some titles have multiple authors while have only one. By contrast, standard business software has brief records and usually short field lengths as well. If the library decides to modifies existing library-or business oriented software, the costs of modification must be projected. These costs, beyond the price of the software, include the programmer, staff time to specify the necessary changes and delayed implementation until the changes are completed.

Changes may also void maintenance contracts and performance guarantees, and future releases are likely to be incompatible. In short, the library must assume total support responsibility, as it must with locally developed systems. Successful adaptation cannot be guaranteed, but a schedule for evaluating the progress of the software changes should be established. Periodic reviews should document all developments and revise the schedule if necessary. The question of ownership must also be addressed.

The original software developer has a significant investment in the programme, but the extent of the changes determines whether or not the software is considered a new product. In-house software development is a major undertaking. However, it may be the only option if there are no existing programmes that meet the library's specifications. In-house development is generally more expensive than purchasing existing software where development costs are spread over several users.

As with modifying software, writing programmes requires

not only programming expertise but also considerable commitment by the entire library to define the exact capabilities of the system. There are also no guarantees that the final product will be the one initially envisioned. Additionally, the system will not be ready immediately; in fact, very few programming efforts for complex applications have stayed on schedule.

Delays result in postponed installation, longer use of the manual or earlier automated system and increased development costs because more staff time is needed. In-house development, as stated before, requires programming expertise. The library must determine if that capability exists among its staff or if additional programmers will be necessary. Even if a staff member can do the programming, someone else must assume that person's regular duties. In-house development also increase the number of hardware options which must be evaluated. Selecting existing software often determines the hardware that can be used or at least reduces the number of micros that can be pondered over.

Maintenance and Enhancement

In fact, development or expansion of a system may have an end, but ongoing maintenance and future enhancements do not. Staff support will be required on a continual basis as the library determines that a few changes are necessary, for example, to speed processing or to make the system more user cordial. Reports never quite seem to meet the desires of the staff after the system is installed—requests for slight format changes or inclusion of additional fields of data are inevitable.

Naturally, the library can stand firm and refuse to consider such changes and enhancements, but one result may be that the system will not be used effectively. Further, as new operating systems become available from the vendors, the library may wish to upgrade the system to improve response time. Existing programmes would then need to be revised for the new operating system. On the whole, it is best to assume that ongoing support costs for both maintenance and enhancement will be part of automation.

System Capabilities Agenda

Whether purchasing software packages, modifying existing programmes or developing the entire system locally, the library should first state its requirements in a written subclassification for the desired system. This document should be extremely detailed. A frequent approach is to label the various functions as mandatory, desirable and "blue sky." For an acquisitions system, for example, printing of purchase orders and fund accounting capabilities may be mandatory.

An online vendor file might be viewed as desirable, while vendour performance statistics on orders filled, time delays and discounts could be considered "blue sky." Naturally, the ranking of different features varies among libraries. The library should also determine how its work environment will affect the performance of the system and should anticipate the impact of various problems or shortcomings. If the system must be stand-alone for a particular function, determine the frequency of that operation.

Can it be scheduled at a time when the system would not otherwise be in use? Consider the trade-offs between various requirements; some capabilities may be possible with larger systems, but the performance may not justify the larger expense. After the library has defined the desired system, an evaluation of existing packages should be made. This should cover each system's probable lifetime, potential for expansion, reliability and documentation.

The evaluation should also include information from both system vendours and users—each has a different perspective, and each reveals different aspects of the system. By objective and fair. When calling other users, talk to both the library administration and the operators who use the system daily. Determine the role and the perspective of the person giving the comments. For example, if there are complaints of recent downtime, ask if that is a frequent occurrence of simply a recent and temporary problem.

If it is the first major problem in two years, it may not be very important, despite the inconvenience at the time. Actual statistics from a broad time period will ensure a true representation of performance. After investigating several systems, the library may recognises a need to revise its specifications. It may find details that were overlooked, or new ideas may have been sparked by the review of existing systems.

Once the functional capabilities of existing systems are known, the library should evaluate each system's probable lifetime. Of course, no system will last forever. The rapid changes in microcomputer technology have two basic impacts: technical support for current systems may be discontinued as new ones are developed, and new technology may eventually make it more efficient for the library to change to a new system. Therefore, the lifetime of a system should be defined as the probable length of time that the system will meet the library's needs.

A small circulation system may not handle the level of activity that the library anticipates after five years, but if it will last that interim period, the system might be amortised and considered a sound investment. Another aspect is whether or not the system can be upgraded through the same vendour.

If the product has many unique characteristics that are tied to the particular micro or its operating system, or if the manufacture of either the hardware or software is not likely to make the future enhancements that you anticipate needing, the library may have considerable problems in transferring to a later system.

This is especially critical in the transfer of data from one system to another. If a new system does not have compatible record formats and file structures, the information may need considerable editing. Creating a data base once is extremely expensive—revising it with every system change would be an economic disaster.

Further, the library must be sure that both hardware and software can be expanded to meet future needs. For example, some systems allow for single stations, while others support multiple terminals. The library should check that the software structure does not prevent adding more indexes or changing the record structure to variable-length fields. The storage capacity of some system cannot be expanded as the data base grows; some may not support hard disks, causing a problem if it becomes necessary to progress beyond the limited storage capacity and reliability of floppy disks. System expandability also involves issues of compatibility among microcomputers and possibly with larger computers when there is a desire to link systems. Some microcomputer vendours have developed higher-level systems that are not compatible with their own more basic systems; therefore the system cannot be upgraded to the larger computer even though it comes from the same vendour.

Despite the dynamic state of the microcomputer industry, problems of compatibility are not likely to be resolved in the immediate future. The library must also determine what peripheral devices can be added to a system. For example, some system do not have letter quality printers, which may be needed initially or planned for the future. Even though a library may not need all the various options and possible capabilities, the selection evaluation should determine what future alternatives do exit.

How Much Reliable?

Reliability should be considered on two levels: the performance of the entire system and that of each component. This is important both in defining whether or not the system is meeting the contractual requirements and in evaluating existing installations. The microcomputer may function, but if the terminal or printer is down, work cannot be done. If the system configuration supports multiple work stations, one terminal may be available while another is not. People have different definitions as to what constitutes the system being down—and vendours tend to consider the system to be working unless the entire configuration is not operational. Concern over system reliability seems to vary among librarians, probably depending on their experiences with technology. A system's performance, however, will have a critical effect upon efficiency, staff acceptance and the library's ability to provide services.

In evaluating system reliability at existing installations, it is important to determine whether or not the environment is similar to that of your own library. Much heavier or lighter work loads can have a major effect on performance, as can the size of the data base being supported and the number of terminals used. Analyse the technical expertise of other users. Is it similar to your own?

Is their success or failure due to their own capabilities or misconceptions, rather than to the particular system they are using? Standardise your definitions of terms such as response time and downtime, and be specific. Adjectives such as "fast" or "poor" are relative—determine the number of seconds for various types of functions.

Documentation

The documentation of any system, regardless of type of computer, is crucial to its success and should be valuated carefully. Good documentation is difficult and expensive to write, and it is not readily found. Preparing documentation is likely to be even more of a problem for small companies than for larger ones, which have entire departments of technical writers devoted to producing promotional and descriptive literature.

Basically, documentation must be complete and understandable at all levels—programming, user manuals and hardware. Programming documentation may be the major issue if you will support the system yourself. It is impossible to take on the support or enhancement of existing programmes without understanding how they operate. User documentation is equally important to the success of the system, although it is possible for the library to develop or enhance this type of aid if necessary.

Even if user documentation is available, the library may wish to customise it somewhat. For that purpose, programming documentation is again important for purchasing a package since it provides background to understanding the system and subsequently preparing the user manuals. Hardware documentation is generally standard and available from the manufacturer, either directly or through a second vendour if your purchase a package of software and hardware together.

The major point to watch for is documentation of any hardware modifications by the second vendour. Foe example, terminals may be modified or the bus structure changed to facilitate a particular software package. Such modifications mean that the original manufacture will not provide any maintenance on that hardware—the buyer must rely on the company that made the modifications. Should that second firm go out of business or discontinue that particular piece of hardware, future maintenance can be a problem. In such a case, documentation is extremely important to enable a third party to assume maintenance. (However, this can be very expensive, as the third party will charge for its learning time.)

The decision to purchase a microcomputer system obviously requires an analysis of the costs involved. As part of the needs assessment, a cost analysis of the current operations should be done to compare with the cost of installing and operating the computer. Costs can be divided into four categories; all must be considered in determining the library's ability to support the system. Initial purchase price and ongoing support and staff costs are discussed in this section. Site preparation and transfer of data from the existing system to the new one are discussed in the sections that follow.

The basic cost of buying a microcomputer plus peripherals is generally the one looked at first. The changes in microcomputer technology have resulted in decreasing costs, making such systems affordable for more and more libraries. As indicated elsewhere, micro-processor chips have rapidly dropped in price and predictions are that the trend will continue. Some peripherals are still quite expensive, but they too are showing a downward trend. Cost analysis should consider the base system that can meet current needs and the costs for enhancing the system if there are plans to expand its use by adding other applications or accommodating more users. Such expansion would require more terminals or storage capacity. The library should develop a timetable for anticipated expansion; if it will take place within two years, expansion costs should be considered and compared among the systems being considered. If expansion is not likely for another five years, then the probability of upgrading the current system is low.

Technological advances will probably make a change to an entirely new system ore appropriate. If the existing system is upgraded in several years, the costs are likely to be quite different that for the same enhancements at current prices. However, because the library may recognise many possible expansions once the system is installed, information on expansion possibilities and costs should be part of any cost analysis. When evaluating systems, consider the costs of hardware and software separately. This facilitates comparisons with other systems, even if the hardware and software are marketed as a combined system package.

Software could be purchased from another library, a private consultant or a retail store, as well as from a system vendor. Knowing the costs of each component of the system enables the library to project future costs for adding more tape drives, terminals, etc. While there are relatively few microcomputer-based "package systems" that specify prices for hardware, software, maintenance and future enhancements, they are starting to emerge. It is important to know the cost of each component as well as overall price in comparing different systems with similar ability to satisfy the library's needs. In such packages, the vendor may cover overhead costs, future maintenance support and profits through inflated hardware prices.

While that is a valid approach, it is important to see where these costs are being covered. Depending upon whether they are included in the ongoing maintenance fee or in the hardware component prices, the ongoing costs and the future costs of expanding the system are affected. The vendor should also be asked to provide costs for adding various components, including some that may not be part of the initial system. Maintenance costs for both hardware and software should be quoted. Many library packages based on mainframes and minicomputers have been marketed with the understanding that future enhancements will be distributed in later releases of the software. If this is the case with a micro system, then the costs should be stipulated.

While the initial purchase costs are important budget considerations, they are often mistaken as the primary costs of automation. Most likely, the ongoing costs of supporting and using the system will exceed the initial dollar investment; thus, the consideration of ongoing costs is very important in preparing the cost justificarion of the system. Hardware, software and vendor-produced package systems may have monthly maintenance fees. Some software packages have license fees since the proprietary rights are not released.

Naturally, any system requires supplies such as paper and forms, floppy disks or cassettes, and print wheels and tapes. While these expenses are generally much lower than those for hardware or software, they should be compared among various systems. The impact of a new system on the library staff is a frequently overlooked cost. Staff productivity is affected during the preparing, installing, testing, debugging and training for a new system. Possible reorganisation of duties and work procedures takes time to define and implement.

New procedure manuals may be necessary, several staff members may require training, and new problems may need to be addressed. These are all part of the initial costs and presumably cease once the system is functioning properly, but it is important to realise their impact. Libraries that elect to develop their own microcomputer software face significant ongoing costs in personnel salaries. As discussed earlier, even if the software is developed by someone already on the staff, the library is paying that salary, which must then be attributed to the cost of the system. That is true even if that person's previous responsibilities are absorbed by other personnel, incurring no new or increased salary expenditures. Depending upon the complexity of the programmes, the amount of time for software development could vary from a matter of days to several months.

If the software is developed locally, it will probably be maintained in-house as well, Any future changes, improvements or correction of "bugs" will continue to require staff hours. While it would be possible to contract for outside maintenance, a new programmer must learn the package before making any changes or corrections; thus, the library pays for the learning time whenever someone new is introduced. A similar situation exists if the library support staff is replaced. If the programmes were written by a staff member who was not classified as a programmer, the library may need a programmer when he leaves, and this may be a higher level staff position. A full-time, trained programmer may also be advisable if the library plans a complex system in terms of programme sophistication.

As discussed under needs assessment, one purpose of automation may be to reduce staff costs, but a programmer may be more expensive than the clerical staff replaced by the system. The needs assessment and the library's dependence upon the system must be considered in planning the support arrangements. The greater the impact the system has on the library, the more important and justifiable the support of the system by a full-time programmer.

Generally, microcomputers have been hailed as eliminating all the environmental requirements of the larger computers. It is true that the small micros do not generate enough heat to require supplemental air conditioning, and they do not need special wiring. However, the larger microcomputer systems—those that can support large data bases and multiple users—are more susceptible to heat and power fluctuations. Site specifications from the hardware manufacturer should be studied carefully.

Systems that support multiple terminals at various locations will need to have coaxial cable strung from the computer to the different sites. If holes are needed in walls or floors, the library may have to hire a carpenter. The use of the system and its impact on work-flows may even result in some remodeling of work areas. Larger desks or lower tables may need to be purchased to accommodate terminals.

Many of the gains made through automation require changing the approach to accomplishing a task rather than simply imitating the earlier procedures with a computer. However, applications that involve the transfer of data from one system to another pose an additional set of problems and incur additional costs. Manual files of on-order materials or records of materials cataloged and indexed over the last several years need to be keyed into the new system. Such a project can consume many man-hours and may require additional staff during the implementation period. If the library has the information in machine-readable form from another system, it will undoubtedly be more efficient to transfer the data directly into the new system. (The capability of the system to accept machine-readable data should have been considered in the functional analysis of systems during the selection process.)

For data on either cassettes or floppy disks, the local system must have the appropriate peripherals to read them. If the file is on larger machine tapes, the best alternative would probably be to download the data to the micro system, since the tapes and disks of the larger machines cannot be mounted on microcomputers for data transfer. Regardless of how data are transferred, the format of the data must be considered. Record formats may change periodically, and programmes must be modified to reflect the changes. This requires programming expertise as well as a knowledge of present and future data formats and any unique characteristics of the data treatment.

It is remarkable to note here that microcomputer systems are available from numerous sources: directly from the manufacturer; from computer shops, which deal in numerous products; from other libraries; and from vendours who have modified the hardware or created specialised packages of hardware and applications software. Whatever the source, the library needs to consider vendour characteristics that can affect future satisfaction with the system.

Many microcomputer firms have already come and gone. Many current hardware and software products will probably disappear gradually as the market is taken over by a few major companies. No one can predict which ones will succeed or fail, but libraries should be aware of each company's financial stability when selecting a system. Ask how many systems have been sold. Contact libraries with existing installations to determine the vendor's reputation for backing the product. It is especially important to evaluate the vendour's commitment to the product if you are dealing with a small independent company or with a new or small division of a larger corporation.

Ask the number of employees. Determine if there are separate staffs to support the management, product development, sales training and maintenance aspects. The downfall of many small companies that have developed microcomputer hardware and software is that everything depends on one or two people, especially if the company started as a side effort rather than a full-time job. Someone capable of designing new hardware or software is not necessarily a good manager or marketing person. Also, if his interests change and he abandons the product for another one, the company may not have anyone capable of providing support or maintenance. This is not to say that all microcomputers and software from small shops should be avoided. Some very good products are available through them, and many of the successful microcomputer systems being marketed to libraries today began under similar conditions. However, the library should consider what alternatives if has should the company discontinue its product. In some cases, a system will involve more than one vendour or manufacturer. The hardware and software may not be from the same source, and each may be marketed by a retail store rather than by the company that made the computers or wrote the programmes. This can make it difficult to get an expert explanation of the capabilities of the system. Salesmen in general computer stores that retail machines and software packages are usually not oriented toward specialised applications. They may be hardware specialists, programmers or marketing staff.

Because few library packages are sold through retail stores, and few salesmen have library background, salesmen tend to promote general package products. Usually with such packages, either the programmes or the library procedures must be modified or compromised. Remember that it is the librarian's responsibility to learn what is available and decide if existing programmes are appropriate. Most library-specific packages are coming from people or companies who understand libraries and information centers.

Many have been developed by library staff or by programmers under the direction of librarians. In these cases, the salespeople may have aided in the development or have access to those who did. Since they are dealing with comparatively few packages, they are well-versed in the capabilities and the types of environments where the packages would be used. These companies are also more likely to include future system enhancements through periodic software releases. In some cases, this option may be tied into the maintenance contracts.

Software is also available from libraries that have developed their own programmes. Some libraries trade or give away software; others sell it to recoup some of the development costs. When obtaining software from another library, it is important to find out how much assistance the library will provide with the programme. Will user instruction and programming assistance be offered? How complete is the documentation, both for programmers and for users? Libraries are most likely to offer their software as an operational system but with no guarantee that problems will not arise if new conditions or types of data are introduced.

The receiving library should make clear whether it wishes to make changes in the software and whether or not it has the programming expertise to understand the programme and make modifications. The original library should clarify whether the software is copyrighted and whether the second library may, in turn, give away or sell its programmes. As with commercially available programmes, there are several other questions to be considered. Will the modifications change the ownership? Will there be future releases and enhancements? If so, how will they be distributed to other users of the programme?

Maintenance support is another important consideration in evaluating a dealer or agency. Usually for micro hardware maintenance, the owner must ship equipment to the vendour or take it to the store where purchased. On-site maintenance is unlikely except for some of the largest micros. If a vendour marketing a combination hardware/software package is willing to provide such support, it will be very expensive, proportional to the total system costs. Plane fares to the site or staff time to perform the repairs cost the some for a micro as for the more expensive minis and mainframes. The maintenance available for microcomputers varies according to the size of the computer. Naturally, the smaller the size and thus the lower the price of the hardware, the lower the maintenance support the company can afford to provide. Maintenance by computer store staff will vary significantly from one shop to another, depending upon the size of the store and the level of support staff it can afford. Generally, there is more profit in sales than in maintenance and most vendours are likely to concentrate their resources on the former.

In fact, Software purchased through retail stores may have similar problems of maintenance support. Relatively few library-specific applications are being sold through retail shops, but general word processing or accounting routines used by libraries are available and frequently require little or no maintenance. An additional problem of retail software is that expandability, resolution of flaws or any further enhancements may not be covered.

Though they may be guaranteed to perform certain functions, such programmes are frequently viewed as one-time development efforts. Maintenance of software by vendours may include continual phone support to answer questions, decipher error messages or solve programme bugs; or it may specify a limited amount of consultation on such problems. Extremely complex problems could result in on-site visits by either software or hardware engineers. Remote diagnostics via phone links to the local system are another possibility. Regardless of the type of support, maintenance is an ongoing expense for the vendour, who must retain staff for as long as the system is supported. This will be reflected in the purchase price and ongoing maintenance fees.

Relative to the cost of the hardware and software, this cost may seem unreasonably high. However, once again, support staff salaries, maintenance equipment and operating expenses are not significantly different from those supporting application packages on larger, more expensive machines. As with hardware, the ratio of ongoing maintenance cost to software purchase price is much higher for micro systems.

Vendors may distribute upgraded software after design or programming flaws are discovered. Some vendours perceive their product as an ongoing, evolving package, and any errors found by users will be corrected and redistributed. Others consider the development a single project with a beginning and ending date; once accepted by the library, the programmer has no more responsibilities.

A major issue in the selection of any system is the contract. Contract terms and considerations will depend on the size of the purchase and on whether the contract covers hardware, software or a package of both. Hardware is generally sold with standard warranties or contracts regarding its capabilities and the type of maintenance support that will be provided. No guarantees of application software performance will be made by the hardware vendour if software is purchased separately. Instead, system capabilities will be defined in terms of number of terminals that the microcomputer can support, the types and amounts of storage, the languages and operating systems that can be used and the type of printer. Much of the discussion here will therefore concentrate on contracts for either software or complete packages containing both hardware and software. In either case, a contract is extremely important. It is the library's only assurance that the product will perform as described—and its only protection if it does not. Only written agreements and guarantees are enforceable. For this reason, the contract should be considered very carefully rather than as an afterthought or as the final procedure of system procurement.

Naturally, however, the library must consider the size of the purchase in developing a contract; the greater the dollar expenditure, the more important the contract for both the library and the vendour. For system packages that include both software and hardware, the contract must clearly identify who is responsible for rectifying any problems. Buying a system from a single vendour is the simplest approach since the vendour, not the library, is then responsible for identifying whether a problem is hardware—or software-based. The vendour should be held responsible for meeting the contract's specifications for remedying problems within a certain amount of time. Libraries that buy hardware and software separately or whose contract does not specify a single party as responsible for resolving difficulties should recognise the problems that may arise with determining maintenance responsibility.

The contract should specify in detail a product description, acceptance criteria, the test period, payment terms and maintenance agreements. Although the library should not be skeptical about the system it purchases, it is best to approach the contract development phase with the assumption that problems will be a normal part of implementation. With a detailed contract, both library and vendour will have a clearer understanding of what the library wants, what the system can provide and what action will be taken in various situations. This understanding promotes more successful implementation and use of the system.

The system profile or product description can be from the vendour or the library. It may be the original or a revised specification document prepared by the library, especially if a bid process is used for the procurement. The contract's product description should address hardware and software (if it covers both).

Exact hardware components should be identified, along with their capabilities. The contract may include reference to specific manufacturer descriptions. If the hardware has been modified by the vendour, those changes should be described in detail. Software descriptions should contain a detailed analysis of the functional capabilities and, of course, should meet the library's requirements. Capabilities should be well-defined rather than stated in generalities.

If there are specific requirements as to how a function is performed, in addition to the fact that it is supported by the system, these must be stated. For example, the phrase "online editing" does not specify if an entire field must be re-entered to correct a spelling error or if an omitted letter can simply be inserted by cursor positioning. Such descriptions may be made jointly with the vendor; both parties must agree on the description. In addition to detailing the functional capabilities that the system must support, the document should specify performance criteria. Response time, data base size, quality of print products and functions to be supported simultaneously are good examples of aspects that can be specified.

Performance criteria must also consider the impact of

other variables: for example, whether response time will decrease with multiple terminals or a larger data base; or whether report generation programmes can run simultaneously with online editing if more terminals are added or if different storage devices are used.

The contract should define the acceptance tests that will be performed on the system. The length of the test period should be stated. The type of application and the sophistication of the system will be the primary factors in establishing the length of the test, but the library should also require a lengthy amount of time if implementation and training are complex.

If a data base is involved, for example, the system will probably not provide accurate performance statistics until that file is loaded and all simultaneous work stations are operational. The vendour should realise that system capabilities may not be fully appreciated if the staff is not yet well trained and comfortable. If the system supports multiple functions, all should be tested. In order to determine typical response times, various workloads should be simulated and documented. Collect enough data to determine a statistically valid average and indication of the maximums and minimums.

Define response time and the test parameters for applications such as a circulation system or a retrieval package. For example, is response time measured from the time the enter key is pressed until the data begin to appear on the screen or until the entire retrieved information is displayed? Indicate the size of the files, the number of simultaneous users and any other variables that could affect the test results. Then change the type of transaction or the number of users and repeat the tests. If certain functions will be done simultaneously, test them simultaneously.

If reports can be printed while the data base is loading or

the terminals are active, determine the performance under those conditions and any other environments likely to be needed once the system is being used. Acceptance testing may also affect when payment will be made, and this should be stated in the contract. If the acceptance test must be passed before payment, the length and details of the test are even more important. The library will have for more leverage in receiving a system that performs as marketed if payment is withheld until the criteria are satisfied. If the system fails the acceptance test, the library can decide whether or not the test period should be extended.

Maintenance and Service

As is obvious from the preceding discussion, various maintenance options may be offered by the different sources of hardware and software. The contract should specify the type of maintenance support in detail. It should include turnaround time for responding to maintenance requests, such as a guarantee to arrive on site within a given number of hours after being notified of a system problem. If there is no on-site maintenance, the contract should state how quickly various problems will be corrected once the equipment is delivered to the vendour. The library must determine whether it will require the vendour to lend or rent other equipment if the library's equipment must be repaired. For example, a circulation system terminal may be more indispensible than one used for data entry or for producing purchase orders because the latter processes do not involve general library users.

The contract can stipulate that identical equipment will be loaned or may allow for comparable machines to be substituted if they are available. If the system is purchased as a vendour package, complete with ongoing maintenance, the contract may tie software maintenance to future enhancements. Problems and programme errors may be resolved in a new updated release of the system that also contains additional system capabilities. In this case, the library should clarify the frequency and the means of determining whether a desired improvement or change will be made. The contract should also address modifications made to the purchased package by the library. Changes made by the library will generally void any maintenance agreement or performance guarantees since the original developer cannot be responsible for the level of work being performed. Changes will also be likely to render the system incompatible with any future updates or releases that the vendour may provide.

Software Development

Practically, contracting for customised software development is very difficult. Specifications of the desired product must be extremely detailed since differing interpretations of a function can lead to an unacceptable system. The contract must stipulate various benchmarks or progress reviews to help ensure that the product is developing in the right direction. Otherwise, misunderstandings may not be recognised until the product is delivered. The contract must state penalties or planned action should the product fail to meet the specifications or deadlines for completion.

These must be amended, however, if the library changes the system requirements once development has started. Future support of the product should also be outlined. If a programmer develops the product as a one-time contract, the library will probably have to provide its own maintenance support or at least contract with another vendour. The contract should also state ownership in such cases.

Since the library is paying for the development, it has some claim to complete ownership and rights to the programmes once delivered. The library should consider the contract as part of its process of evaluating existing systems and should write its own agreement terms in order to protect its interests. Then, after deciding what requirements are important and what the contract should accomplish, the library should examine other contracts, including those offered by the vendour.

Undoubtedly, overlooked issues will be found, and the contract will need revisions. However, this approach avoids the pitfalls of simply accepting a vendour contract without realising points that it may omit. Purchasing a computer system is generally a large expenditure, and the library is in a position to negotiate the contract, especially for larger systems. The vendour may be flexible on discounts, maintenance or other benefits. However, the library must be realistic. The number of available packages and the size of the purchase are the two primary factors in negotiating the purchase, and both the library and the vendours know the marketplace.

FURTHER Many libraries hire a consultant to assist in selecting an automated system. This may be important if the library has no expertise among its staff for evaluating automated systems. However, the library should determine the exact role that the consultant will play. It should select a consultant whom it respects and trusts. However, the consultant is only an advisor; the library is still responsible for the final decisions. To be truly effective in the selection of a system, the consultant should be involved in the project from the beginning. The library should determine what it wants to automate and the basic requirements of a system.

Once that has been a accomplished, the consultant can assist in a needs assessment, giving objective comments on existing procedures. He may also be able to provide information on features other libraries have found desirable, may be more aware of existing system capabilities and may have a more realistic approach to what should be sought. Using a consultant in selecting a microcomputer system is somewhat similar to purchasing a maintenance contract for the system: both may seem too expensive relative to the price of the actual system. However, the amount of time and expertise required to select a micro system is a function of system sophistication, not the size and cost of the computer. The impact on the library in terms of service, costs and operations will have to be considered to determine if the added costs of a consultant are justified. If a consultant is retained, it is advisable to have a contract that details what the library will do and what will be delegated to him. The contract should state the amount of time that the consultant should provide, written reports or documents that are to be submitted, the types of advice that are to be provide and payment agreements etc.

Procurement options with microcomputers are somewhat different from those of systems based on larger computers. Many of the packages are developed by small companies or by single individuals who have neither the time nor inclination to respond to Request for Proposal (RFP) documents or to engage in competitive bidding for a contract or sale. In these cases, the sole option is direct purchase. However, as more microcomputer applications are developed, it is likely that more companies will undertake active marketing programmes and begin responding to bid requests.

Libraries must determine first if they are required to use the bid process; many publicly supported libraries, whether academic or city, must use this procedure. However, if there is an option, the pros and cons must be considered. The bid process of issuing an RFP, evaluating the responses and selecting a system may help obtain the desired system at a lower price. However, the process itself is expensive and time-consuming. The library should evaluate the existing marketplace. If there are very few systems that perform the exact functions required, the bid process may not be necessary.

To conclude, size and cost of a system, as well as its intended function in the library, should determine the amount of time and effort that go into the selection process. It is not cost-effective to spend several months of staff time to select a system that costs a few hundred dollars and that will be used to experiment with microcomputers.

On the other hand, a system that will result in a total restructuring of work procedures or will dramatically alter library use patterns must be chosen carefully. Its success will be important to the library's continued viability. Most systems fall between these two extremes, and the library must determine the system impact, resulting costs and the appropriate selection concerns as part of the initial needs assessment while finally deciding for.

5

Professionalism in Service Providing

"Zeal without knowledge is like fire without a grate to contain it; like a sword without a hilt to wield it by; like a high-bred horse without a bridle to guide him. It speaks without thinking, acts without planning, seeks to accomplish a good end without the adeption of becoming mean."

—**Julius Bate**

Here we intend to advance a conceptual framework for considering library services. It is not asserted that what follows constitutes a complete framework, but rather an attempt to take a step toward the development of a framework. The motivation is both intellectual and pragmatic. At an intellectual level, there is curiosity about the nature of things and about how—and why—they work. At a pragmatic level, there is the incentive that a clearer theoretical understanding might bring greater effectiveness in practice.

No doubt, theory brings insights, but there is no guarantee that theory will be helpful in practice. Bad theory may bring false and misleading insights, good theory brings helpful insights. However, theory, once developed, can, in general, be tested—and inadequate theory rejected. A necessary condition for progress, then, is to propose theory so that it can be tested.

While providing services to library users some questions arise in our mind, like—

(a) Why do library services differ from each other from one context to another?

(b) How do the different facets of librarianship relate to one another?

(c) What is "goodness" with respect to library services?

(d) How do libraries survive?

(e) How big should a library be?

(f) How should catalogs and retrieval systems be evaluated?

(g) Why aren't libraries used more?

It is asserted that it is lack of theory which causes these questions to be and to remain—problems.

It is remarkable to note that there are five key aspects of the provision and use of library services which include:

(a) Inquiries
(b) Retrieval
(c) The process of becoming informed
(d) The demand for library services
(e) The allocation of resources to and within library services.

Although an evenly balanced overview is desirable, some topics must be given more attention than others. This unevenness derives from two considerations:

(a) The development of theory with respect to library services is itself uneven. For example, little seems to be known about how users come to formulate the inquiries which they bring to libraries.

(b) Some topics need a longer and more careful exposition than others in order to describe them adequately.

Not only does the state of theory concerning library services hardly seem ready for such treatment but, even if it were, formal, rigorous treatment would probably have hindered communication with many people who would otherwise have been interested.

We are concerned with library services and, therefore, with both the provision and the use of these services. The intent has been to focus on the theoretical aspects and the emphasis is on developing a framework—on how the parts fit together and into the context in which the services are provided. Indeed, a suitable subtitle would have been "Toward a conceptual framework for considering the structure and functioning of library services in relation to their sponsors, their users, and their societal context."

Most of the literature about library services has to do with specific details such as indexing, classification, logistics, and social mission. It is clearly important to have such detailed treatments. In contrast, however, the pages that follow represent an attempt to provide a general theoretical framework. Ideally, the more specialized theoretical work will fit within and into this more general treatment. The one should complement the other.

Circulation Functions

In fact, circulation of books is the pivotal role of a library. The activities of the circulation department involve giving assistance to users in using the catalogue; issuing and receiving books; maintaining borrowers' records; keeping records and statistics; conducting studies of the use of library materials; collecting fines; and formulating policies and procedures for these activities.

The circulation section is, therefore, the most important part of the library and its functions are as follows:

1. To enrol members for the library.
2. To issue books for home reading, official work or otherwise to the borrowers/readers/officials through their borrowers tickets/Passbooks or requisition slips.
3. To maintain shelf arrangement.
4. To get the suggestions of the readers for the purchase of books and arrange their purchase through Acquisition section.
5. To issue No Demand/Clearance Certificates to the members at the time of their leaving the library membership.
6. To recall overdue books/material.
7. To maintain statistics on the working of the Division.
8. To reserve books/material which have been requested.

Further circulation section usually consists of three parts:

(a) the issue desk where books are charged and discharged, requests and general enquiries are attended to.

(b) the work room where routines such as sending reminders, handling inter-library loans and servicing readers' requests are undertaken.

(c) the shelves, equipment area.

Most of these tasks require the adoption of a definite issue system on "charging" following certain routines and promoting efficiency. The libraries of earliest times kept simple records in the registers/ledgers when closed access was there. With the expansion and diversification of library materials the use of the library increased, the open access was introduced and new charging systems were invented. For the last several decades various systems have come into use.

First of all, book card file systems such as Browne and Newark were predominant. Then came the Transaction Card File systems with Mechanisation and the Photo-charging systems. Finally, the contemporary technological societies of the developed countries have made strides with the most advanced mechanical device in this field—the Computer.

No single issue system is ideal for all Library situations. While choosing a system, a library has to take into account its own peculiarities. Cost, speed, simplicity, accuracy, security and circulation activities are some of the factors in choosing a system.

The main issue systems are as follows:

1. Browne
2. Newark
3. Bookamatic
4. Photocharging
5. Multiple issue slip system
6. Token charging
7. Computers.

The photocharging system is now most common in many Indian libraries. Except Browne none of the other systems is popular. In some Indian libraries the circulation of books is done through computer's application.

Browne System

Since this system is most popular, it is necessary to explain it in detail. In this system the borrower is given a ticket called Borrower's Ticket in the form of a pocket bearing his/her name and address. The loan is effected by (a) placing the book card each in the borrower's ticket and filing it by date due, sub-arranged by accession number, author or the call No., (b) stamping the book with the date of return. When the book is returned the discharge is effected by

(a) Noting the date due;
(b) searching and retrieving the loan record from the issue file;
(c) separating the book card from the borrower's ticket;
(d) putting the card back in the book and returning the ticket to the borrower.

Merits

The advantages of the system are: (i) Charging is relatively rapid, (ii) the reader does not participate, (iii) errors in the loan are minimum, (iv) economical on stationery, (v) simple to operate and overdues are easily located.

Demerits

In this system main disadvantages are that discharging is slow and only single record of loan is kept. Despite its shortcomings Browne system is really an ideal system for small and medium-sized libraries. With modification, it can be used in almost any type of library.

Registration of Borrowers

For borrowing books for outside the library reading, the readers are registered within rules and regulations of the library. Reader has to fill up the application form providing his or her particulars. Most of the libraries require the signature of a responsible person and in case of government libraries the signature of administrative authority under whose control the reader is working. The application form should be as simple as possible though there cannot be a same form for every type of library, yet the basic information required to be entered in the form is the same.

It is pertinent to note that Public libraries are open to all the readers but in other types of libraries the membership is restricted to special type of clientele.

Rules

The readers should be asked to read the rules of the library before they are registered as borrowing members of the library.

Reminders

Reminders for overdue books from the borrowers should be sent in time.

Shelving

Shelving of books in a library is most important part of the circulation section. Books should be restored on the shelves as soon as they are returned. The shelving should be accurate and tidy. Once in a while the shelf-reading should be done to see that the books are properly arranged in correct order.

Inter-Library Loans

No doubt, no library is self-sufficient. More often than not there are occasions in a library when books are obtained from other libraries on inter-library loan. The book asked for by the user for urgent use can either be purchased or obtained from other libraries. Even if the book is not out of print and is available in the market, it takes time to get it and to make available to the user. In such situation the library has to borrow book immediately on inter-library loan. Efforts should be made to borrow books from sister libraries which are located in the nearest vicinity.

Basically, an inter-library loan is a transaction in which library material, or a copy of the material, is made available by one library to another upon request. Since a library cannot own all materials, inter-library loan is a means of borrowing materials which users need for research and serious study from local, state, or regional libraries. Each library should provide information to library users regarding the purpose of inter-library loan and the library's inter-library loan policies.

The inter-library loan is not one way. The library has also to loan to other libraries. This should be done with mutual cooperation of libraries and requisition for inter-library loan should be entertained. Rare and reference books may not be loaned.

Requests for Reservation of Books

Generally, except Public Libraries all other libraries reserve books for their clientele, which are out on loan. Where there is lot of demand for reservation of books the formal procedure is adopted. The borrower should be provided with a reservation post-card on which he/she writes the particulars of the required item.

The other side of the post-card is used for the borrowers' address. Each issue system should usually have a built-in device for these reservations.

Shelf Reading

There is need for regular shelf reading in order to provide efficient retrieval of materials. The shelves should be read on a regular basis. Damaged books should be removed for repair and binding. Cleaners/Farashes should clean the shelves, racks and other furniture daily as a matter of routine maintenance.

No Demand/Clearance Certificate

Practically, when a reader leaves the office, college,

university, institution, he/she has to obtain a 'No-Demand' Certificate for the clearance of his/her dues. The readers of Public Libraries may not need such Library's 'No Demand' Certificate. In order to streamline the procedure a simple application form (as per *Appendix 5-VIII)* may be duly filled out by the reader. As soon as the application form is received all the necessary records of that particular borrower are crossed and a 'No Demand'/'No Objection/'No Dues/Clearance Certificate is issued to him/her.

Reference Service

The reference service means helping the readers in their use of the library. It is the reference service that builds the reputation of the library. If a good and efficient reference service is provided to the clientele the usefulness of the library is recognised. Whatever the size of the library, it will receive queries of one kind or the other from the readers, which must be answered promptly within the resources of the library. Some questions can be answered immediately by simple consultation but in some cases, a search has to be made which takes time.

Some pertinent questions may be.

1. *Short Range Questions:* Questions requiring simple consultation are called short range questions.
2. *Longe Range Questions:* Questions requiring more time and the use of more than one reference source are normally called long range questions.

Basically, the following factors are very important in delivering quick and efficient reference service:

(a) Capable and skilled staff

(b) Good collection of Reference Sources

(c) Efficient arrangement and maintenance of the collection.

The staff employed in the Reference section should be intelligent, trained in the use of reference books and reference methods and willing to help readers. A skilled reference assistant, who is knowledgeable of reference sources can make a significant difference in the delivery of reference service.

Reference Books

The work of the Reference Section covers everything necessary to help the reader in his/her inquiries including the selection of an adequate and suitable collection of reference books. The possession of the right books and the knowledge of how to use them are essential to the success of a reference section.

There are two kinds of books.

(i) Those which are meant to be read through for either information or enjoyment.

(ii) Those which are meant to be consulted or referred to for some specific piece of information.

Books of the latter kind are called reference books. These are comprehensive in scope, condensed in treatment and are arranged according to some special order to facilitate the ready and accurate finding of information. This special order may be alphabetic, chronological, tabular, regional, classified or systematic. The books which are not arranged in alphabetical order are generally provided with indexes. Alphabetic approach is needed to find a fact or piece of information.

There are some books, which are so comprehensive, accurate and so well provided with indexes though not reference books yet they also serve as reference books. Experience has shown that formal reference books constitute only a part but there are questions and situations where you have to consult other books. Either there is reference in the reference books for such books or the Reference Assistant feels that a particular book might contain the required information. The arrangement and maintenance of the reference collection is very essential. Even if a library has got the best reference collection but if the books can't be retrieved due to lack of shelf reading then what is the use of such a collection. Proper maintenance is equally important. As soon as the new editions of the reference books are available these should be procured to keep the collection uptodate and current. Old editions may be kept aside for reference in times of need.

The reference collection may also be supplemented by adding vertical reference files, indexes and clipping collections. If need be the catalogue may be supplemented by other bibliographic tools depending upon the type of catalogue a library has.

Remarkably, the following books are recommended for reference librarians:

1. Sheehy, E.P. — Guide to Reference Books
2. Katz, W.A — Introduction to Reference Work (2 vols)
3. Cheney, F.W. — Fundamental Reference Sources
4. Walford, A.J. — Guide to Reference Materials

The reference collection of a library should have the following kinds of reference books: Dictionaries, Encyclopaedias, Year Books, Almanacks, Gazetteers, Atlases, Maps,. Bibliographical sources, Directories, Handbooks,

Manuals, Bibliographies, Statistical Sources, Audiovisual sources, Supplements to Encyclopaedias, Guidebooks, Globes, Indexing and Abstracting services.

Standard Reference Books

Standard reference books are essential in a library depending upon its budget and need. There are many more reference books but it is not possible to buy all of them for every library. For example there are more than 1000 Encyclopaedias alone.

Other Services

The librarians should not lose time and opportunity in organising various other services. These services enhance library's role in meeting information needs of its users. The users benefit and are able to save their time in finding information they need. Such services are:

1. *List of New Additions:* A list of new books added to the library may be brought out every month.
2. *Bibliographies:* At regular intervals bibliographies on demand and on topical subject be brought out A bibliography is a list of writings on a given subject or by a given author. As far as possible annotated bibliographies should be brought out. These bibliographies help the readers to provide the background information on the specific subject or author of their interest.
3. *Current Awareness Service (CAS):* It is a system and often a publication for notifying current documents to users of libraries and information services.
4. *Document Back-up:* This service ensures access to documents by the provision of hard copy or microcopy.

The purpose of this service is to provide the needed original document to the clientele.

5. *Article Alert:* Latest articles are brought to the notice of library users according to their subject of interest.
6. *Selective Dissemination of Information (SDI):* It provides location of new items from whatever source to those persons/researchers who need them most in connection with their current work or interest.
7. *Indexing and Abstracting:* These services provide access contents and to information located in books, journals and other publications.

The above services can be organised depending upon the availability of staff and the need of clientele of a library.

Important Steps in Service to Readers

1. Reminders for overdue books should be sent promptly on a regular basis.
2. Readers should be enrolled as members of the library and be given borrowers' tickets.
3. Capable staff with helping nature with pleasant disposition should be employed on the reference service.
4. Books and other library material should be restored on the shelves as soon as returned by users.
5. The arrangement of books on the shelves should be kept in order.
6. Daily dusting and cleaning of books, racks and other furniture should be maintained.
7. Staff deployed on Reference work should be trained in Reference service.

8. Old editions of reference books should be replaced with revised and uptodate editions.
9. Reference books should be kept in helpful order. Shelf reading should be done on a regular basis.
10. A good collection of reference tools should be developed.

MODEL RULES

1. Working Hours

The Library is open on all the days of the year from – A.M. to –– P.M. in summer/winter (Except on——————). These hours may be curtailed or extended in special circumstances by prior notice on the Notice Board.

2. Membership

The membership of the library is open to________and others with permission. All persons, entering the premises of the library, are required to show, on demand, their identity cards to the Janitor at the entrance.

3. Restricted Section

(i) 'Reference and Consultation Books' shall not be lent out of the library.

(ii) Every reader using the reference section of the library shall return the book(s) consulted either to the Librarian or any one of his Assistants at the reference counter before leaving the library.

(iii) Staff of the library working in the reference section will assist readers in locating information and sources on the subject of their study and research.

(iv) Readers in possession of periodicals, reference books etc. should pass them on to any other reader who may require to use them, when such a request is made through any of the library staff members.

(v) If a reader has not finished any book and he wants to continue with it the next day, he should put a slip with his signature and date and inform at the reference desk.

(vi) If a reader wants any pages of a book to be photocopied he should contact the reference desk for permission to get the same photocopied and make payment for the same, if applicable.

4. Borrowing Rights

Books may be borrowed by all members as per rule 2.

(i) Each borrower can borrow_______________books at a time. In exceptional cases, requests for additional books will be considered.

(ii) Books will be loaned for a period of________days.

(iii) Books may be re-issued after the loan period of_______days, if there is no call for it, at the discretion of the Librarian.

(iv) The Librarian can recall any book on loan, if it is required in the library urgently, even if it is not due to be returned.

(v) Sending of reminders is not obligatory for the library.

(vi) No reader shall take a book or journal or any other material out of the library without having it properly issued to him.

5. Inter-Library Loan

No library is self-sufficient in itself. Every library has to augment its collection by borrowing from other libraries. To borrow from other library is known as "Inter-Library Loan

Service." The Library will endeavour to borrow a publication from another library, if the same is not available in the Library. If the same is not returned within the specified time further facilities are likely to be denied. In case of loss, the borrower will have to pay the "replacement cost" fixed by the lending library.

6. Cost of Damaged/Lost Books and Periodicals

(i) If any book or periodical is damaged or lost by the borrower he/she will either replace it or pay its cost. It will have to be replaced by a new book or periodical of the same or later edition, at his/her cost. If the book/ periodical is not available then photocopy and binding charges may be charged from the person who has lost it.

(ii) The price of a rare/out of print book will be determined by the competent authority and it shall be paid by the person responsible for the damage or loss of the book/periodical.

(iii) If a volume from a multi-volume set is lost or damaged the price of the whole set will be charged, unless the volume of the set lost can be obtained separately, in which case the cost of the particular volume alone will be recovered.

7. General Instructions

(i) Every reader entering the library should sign in the visitor's register kept for the purpose at the entrance gate of the library.

(ii) Personal books are not allowed in the library but in certain cases with the permission of the librarian, books may be taken in.

(iii) Writing or making any kind of mark in a book or a periodical is forbidden.

(iv) Cutting or tearing of any photo or page from any publication is prohibited.

(v) Smoking or eating is not permitted in the library.

(vi) Observe complete silence in the library.

(vii) Readers are not allowed to take their belongings inside the library.

(viii) All articles being taken out of the library are subject to inspection at the exit gate.

(ix) It is the responsibility of every borrower to keep the borrower tickets in safe custody. If these are lost, report should be immediately made to the librarian. Duplicate borrower tickets can be had on payment of Rs,_________ if these are lost/damaged.

8. Discipline

(i) All readers are required to observe discipline in the library, and adhere strictly to its rules and regulations.

(ii) The librarian is authorised to terminate the membership of any borrower if he/she is found guilty of misbehaviour.

(iii) Behave with the staff nicely in order to get good and quick service from them.

6

INFORMATION TECHNOLOGY AND LIBRARY DOCUMENTATION

> "There is no such thing as a worthless book, though there are some far worse than worthless; no book that is not worth preserving, if its existence may be tolerate; as there may be some men whom it may be proper to hang, but none who should be suffered to starve."
>
> —**Samuel T Coleridge**

We are living in the age of information and communication technology and our's is a knowledge society. Practically, information technology is defined as the practices and procedures whereby the information processing requirements of the firm's operations are most effectively integrated into the managerial functions.

Now industry has learned that electronic data processing and systems management can be severely limited without sufficient information. In fact, in spite of the computer's almost unbelievable operational speed (micro-seconds and nano-seconds) the limiting factors are the input and output requirements. This input/output restriction places even more importance on information technology. For now, operational information must be planned with the ultimate objective of computer processing in the most efficient and effective manner.

It is not uncommon to find situations where three shifts of key punch operations are scheduled just in order to provide the computer operations with sufficient data for one 8-hour shift. There is one theory in management decision making that contends that what an individual manager will do in an organisation and the quality of the decisions depends on the quality and quantity of information furnished that individual. Information technology is the essence of effective systems management. As is discussed later in the text, the information flow into and out of the various subsystems determines the overall effectiveness of the systems operation.

Consequently, information technology is a double-directional concept. Information is planned and gathered as input for a system; the operational processing of that system then furnishes information output as needed by the other subsystems in the organisation's total system complex. It is altogether appropriate, therefore, that information technology is classed as a discipline, for there are concepts and principles and practices of informational analysis to warrant the restrictions imposed by the discipline connotation. One of the inherent problems associated with information technology is that of restricting information flow. Literally, many managements are simply inundated with paperwork, reports, and information data of all types. One firm became concerned with the number of management reports being prepared and held an elaborate management conference to analyse and screen each report in an effort to reduce the number by elimination or combination. The net result was an increase in the total number, with a monthly report on the reports being prepared.

Consequently, the real, more basic problem becomes one of determining what information the various subsystems managers do need in order to make sound decisions (processing). Because of the computer's capacity for processing data, information technology—i.e., information selectivity—has become a must in systems management. The basic approach to information technology is, by necessity, built around the management processes of planning and controlling via coordination. *Systems planning* is determining basic objectives and the course(s) of action necessary to achieve these objectives. *Systems control* is assuring that the plans are achieved and that the necessary replanning is accomplished. *Systems coordination* is the integration of the planning and controlling operations into a unified systems approach that considers and relates to all others subsystems in the organisation. Decision theory, an offshoot of Taylor's scientific management, is one tool that enables the systems analyst and management to implement concepts of information technology. Decision theory enables information needs to be programmed into three levels associated with the complexity of the system processing design.

These levels are normally considered to be:

(1) highly programmed decisions usually occurring at the lower levels in the organisation where the system processor is more routine and repetitive;

(2) semi-programmed decisions occurring at mid-management levels where exceptions and unusual circumstances are rare but do occur; and

(3) non-programmed decisions occurring at top management levels where considerable unidentified alternatives and analyses are frequently necessary.

Even at the non-programmed level of decision making, there are certain basic information needs that can be and should be programmed and made available for top management when and if needed. Decision theory, together with the discipline of information technology is a primary consideration and a limiting factor in the design and shape of an organisation's systems operations. The manner in which information is collected, analysed, and processed through the various subsystems, together with the managerial practices of delegation and authority will greatly influence the ultimate success of the firm in reaching its goals and objectives.

Computer technology, systems application, and scientific management have combined to foster certain sophisticated developments in information technology. Systems analysis and scientific management are the needs and computer technology is the manner in which this concept is implemented. Information technology embodies four operational techniques: source data automation (SDA), information retrieval (IR), data transmission (DT), and integrated data processing (IDP).

Source Data Automation (SDA)

The objective of SDA is to plan the information requirements so that when the data is first collected in the system it will be captured on a "machine usable form." Machine usable forms should agree with the input language for the computer system, or it will be necessary to convert the original SDA language to a machine usable language in a separate operation.

One of the more typical examples is the capturing of data (SDA) via punched paper tape from such sources as typewriters or cash registers and then converting this punched paper tape language into magnetic tape for computer systems input. While punched paper tape is acceptable as computer input, magnetic tape is much faster, thereby permitting a more efficient utilisation of the computer system. SDA normally assumes eventual computer processing. This is not necessarily so. The concept of SDA or, more simply *data acquisition*, is equally applicable for manual processing operations. The main objective is to systematise the processing system so that whatever data is needed throughout the system is acquired in the most efficient and useful manner as soon as possible. New developments in SDA include punched paper tape, optical character recognition, and magnetic ink character recognition. Punched paper tape was mentioned above, and is a very popular and common method of source data automation. Almost any electrical office machine can be adapted to produce punched paper tape as a by-product of its normal operations.

Certain data can be selected for recording on the punched paper tape, such as totals, sub totals, taxes, or department billings. Punched paper tape is compatible with most data transmission systems, and is an ideal arrangement for collecting data at remote points and then transmittng it to a central computer system for processing.

Optical character recognition (OCR). OCR is a relatively new concept in information technology. Technology itself has been the main reason for delaying the widespread use of OCR. Only in the last few years has OCR becomes economically possible for the smaller more routine data processing activities. There are various techniques employed in the OCR field, but a typical arrangement involves photosensors reading the character (usually a typewritten or printed character, but more recent developments have successfully read handwriting), comparing this photosenthysis to a standard, and then recording the character in some predetermined machine usable language. The typical speed of an OCR system is the reading and recording of about 2400 character per second. Some systems, too, can be programmed to select only key words, or to capture data that is located in a particular section of the form. OCR systems are most typically used by oil companies, utilities, and large credit card systems, where the information can be quickly recorded in account number with the amount involved posted by a machine used at the point of sale. As the technology permits more economic OCR systems, and as the systems professionals research more used of information technology, OCP promises to be one of the largest developing areas of computer and systems application.

Magnetic ink character recognition (MICR). MICR is quite similar to OCR, but it is different on two essential points. One difference is that MICR, depends upon the character being written by a special machine. This prohibits the data to be captured at its source, unless rather expensive equipment is utilised, and the point of sale or other initial recording transaction is altered considerably. The other significant difference is that the MICR characters are not actually read but the amount of magnetic ink used to print each of the character is sensed, and the magnetic force used to determine the value of that character. One of the largest users of MICR language is the banking system. The Federal Reserve System now requires all checks to be printed with the bank's identification code in magnetic ink so that the clearing house operations may be performed on mechanical equipment. An MICR sorter-reader can process up to 57,000 checks per hour. Large banks have begun using magnetic ink recorders to post the amount of each check, or the check itself, so that all remaining operations of accounting and customer statement preparation can be performed by computer processing.

Information Retrieval is a science within itself, the science of semantics. A more correct approach to information retrieval would be information storage and retrieval because the retrieval of information depends largely upon how and in what manner the data was stored in the computer system.

There are at least three limiting factors imposed on information storage and retrieval techniques.

These are: (1) the thinking and verbiage of the original author, (2) the indexer who decides what details will be used in the storage, and (3) the researcher who must understand the manner of thinking and understanding of the author and the indexer. Information storage and retrieval involves indexing and storing vast amounts of data within the computer system and providing the methods whereby all or any part of the data can be recovered quickly in its original form. A concurrent problem associated with computerised information storage and retrieval is that the system works too effectively. It is not uncommon for a researcher to query the computer on a particular subject, and be furnished a list of hundreds of possible sources. It is akin to using the *Reader's Guide* in a library, and then painstakingly following up on each source listed under the desired topic.

The solution to this problem is more effective and scientific indexing and training of the researchers on how to phrase their inquiries. Then, too, some IR systems can be programmed to selectively search for key words, or key phrases, and evaluate the selection by a matrix formula thereby minimising the problem of word choices and connotative meanings.

Data Transmission

In fact, DT perhaps is the most important of all concepts dealing with information technology. Recent developments in the sophisticated use of computer systems equipment would not have been possible without concurrent developments in the transmission of data; i.e., machines talking to machines. Data transmission became a necessity with the large multiplant firms, geographical decentralisation, and the applications of very large scale computing systems in a central location.

Many data transmission systems utilise inexpensive voice grade telephone circuits.

In fact, the Bell System was one of the pioneers in data transmission with the "data phone" to transmit punched card data. Recent developments in the data phone include provisions for punched paper tape and magnetic tape. The aim has been to achieve faster speeds of data transmission—speeds that approach normal computer input speeds, thereby eliminating the extra process and extra equipment of transmitting the data from a transmitter in a remote point to a receiver associated with a computer installation, and then storing the data for later input into the computer system.

Some data transmission facilities permit direct input-output transmission between two or more computer systems at different locations. The distance does not seem to be the problem, for data transmission is required even though the two systems are separated by only one floor of the building.

Integrated Data Processing

Notably, IDP is the cumulative concept dealing with all phases of information technology. IDP is concerned that the source data automation, the data transmission, and the information storage and retrieval processes are most efficiently and effectively coordinated with the computer's operating systems. IDP is not limited to, nor reserved for, application with computerised systems. IDP originated with basic information technology whereby once the data was captured in the firm, by whatever means, the same data could be used many times in subsequent processing operations. Examples of noncomputerised integrated data processing include the sales order, billing invoice, shipping form, and inventory control record—all stemming from the original sales ticket. Integrated data processing is absolutely necessary for the total systems concept, and is quite essential for effective and efficient computer operations. IDP permits greater speed of information handling, contributes to the total systems complex, is highly efficient in reducing costs associated with information technology, and permits great accuracy since the original data is used many times without the data for each operation having to be transferred by human effort.

In fact, information technology is a vital element in computer and systems management, and it is one of the few operations almost totally under local management control. That is, it is the training, development, and the sophistication of systems analysis professionals that determines just what benefits, efficiencies, and advantages will accrue to the organisation from information technology techniques.

AUTOMATIC DATA PROCESSING

It is remarkable to note that two Rand researchers prophesied in a magazine article that:

> ...By 1970, devices for the automatic and semiautomatic entry of data into information systems will be common. Currently, identical information is often repetitively handwritten, then typewritten, then key-punched, and then transferred to magnetic tape for entry into a computer system. Transcription errors as well as duplication of effort inevitably result. Automatic devices, in contrast, accept data directly from the event creating the data, as, for example, when a telephone call automatically (without human intervention) creates and records information as to the origin, destination, and charge for the call. Semiautomatic devices minimize manual involvement in recording data and include, for example, credit card templates.

What is SDA?

In short simple terms, Source Data Automation means

applying automation techniques at the very spot where information originates. Going a little further, John W. Haslett, Shell Oil Company, states that SDA: ... includes the introduction of reliable transaction data at the transaction source and the automatic movement of that data quickly and accurately through all accounting and statistical sequences to develop timely and reliable decision-making information.

SDA has been around for some time. Although the Ford Motor Company used to interchange the term SDA with IDP quite frequently in referring to its paperwork processing, most other management people until a few years ago preferred the term Integrated Data Processing. With today's emphasis on feeding data into computer systems, IDP has become SDA. Both terms call for taking source data at its point of origin and feeding it into an integrated system and out again with a finished product. With SDA a computer is usually involved, which reduces human intervention to a minimum. In private industry, after electronic computers began to demonstrate that they were not "gadgets" but management tools here to stay, executives such as Alan O. Mann began to reexamine the problems associated with data preparation:

> It is apparent then, that these characteristics of industrial data lead us to seek integration. These factors make us conclude that our data processing is not yet integrated. Our data is not sufficiently timely. It is periodic, even though out actual operations are not. We hunt for pennies while thereby expending dollars. Our data is arbitrarily compartmentalised—even though it needs to be unitised to fulfill our company's avowed single purpose of manufacturing and selling its products at a profit. Herein lie the needs for integrated data processing.

Advantages

The decision for choosing Source Data Automation

techniques to resolve paperwork management problems can be supported by these advantages:

1. Elimination of repetitive operations through automatic reproduction of data at all levels of reporting.
2. Speeding up the processing of data through the mechanisation of source data at its *point of origin.*
3. Purification of data through controlled input and automatic movement of data.
4. Utilisation of personnel more effectively by reducing routine work, which in turn:
   (a) Enhances morale and
   (b) Encourages employees to apply their skills in an analytical rather than a clerical capacity.
5. Information availability to management on a more complete and timely basis because the use of pre-verified input media together with increased processing capabilities makes it more practical to record additional useful data at point of origin.

No difficulty usually exists in spotting an area where SDA technique might be applied to improve a work situation. Whenver there is duplication of effort, a growing rate of errors, rarely met deadlines, operations in the system which act as bottlenecks, too huge a volume of work for any manual processing, and many dollars spent continuously on overtime, then there is a need for SDA.

A Model System

Customers send in orders to the company by telephone, purchase order, or personal contact. Next, the expediter batches the orders in the most economical manner, and then gives them to a machine operator.

The operator goes to the files to pull our customer and product data which may be in the form of a deck of EAM cards, edged cards, paper tape, or magnetic tape or cards. A typical customer card will contain customer's name, address, credit rating, salesman's code number, customer code number, and other data. The product card might contain quantity, size, item name, unit price, and extended price for the quantity involved.

A SDA stored programme using a small computer would then perform these operations:

1. Print out transaction documents.
2. Computer, punch, and store required totals.
3. Compare cash totals for accuracy.
4. Fulfill billing requirements in the first writing of invoices.
5. Select out, punch, and communicate transaction detail summary data for central large-scale computer processing of sales and statistical reports.
6. Print out sales, stock level and control reports.

In milliseconds, a small computer can print out a combination invoice and bill of lading, plus other by-products.

Although the small computers serving as part of an SDA system perform yeoman service, they should not be confused with their mammoth big brothers which possess high speeds and huge memory capacities. Remember that the small computer has its limitations in memory, size, speed, flexibility, and in its inability to easily expand to a larger memory capacity. Nevertheless, it has its rightful place in SDA.

Many applications of SDA techniques can be found both in public and private management today. Perhaps one of the most far-reaching applications of SDA in the Federal Government will be that of adapting the Standard Form 50, "Notification of Personnel Action," to mechanised processing. Millions of these basic input documents are processed in the Government each year to show personnel actions affecting employees ranging from recording promotions to showing transfer of duty stations.

Charles J. Sparks, chief, Management Systems Division, U.S. Civil Service Commission, worked out the tremendously difficult task of getting acceptance from the hundreds of Federal agencies for the use of this new form. Sparks, writing in the *Civil Service Journal*, says:

> To facilitate the use of ADP equipment and to achieve a greater standardisation of personal inputs, the Commission has revised this form (SF 50) in collaboration with agencies....... The form was also designed for possible future use on optical character recognition machines—that is, machines that will be able to "see" and "read". This is the first time in history that a standard form for government-wide use has been designed for Source Data Automation.

On the local government level, SDA is being applied, too. In the State of California, unemployment insurance operations are largely mechanised. Claimants are issued an edge-punched identification card. When they file a claim, they present their card to a clerk, who types in the amount of the check. A benefit check is produced and at the same time a record is made on paper tape. At the close of the day, the local office sends the paper tape to a computer center elsewhere in the state for processing.

The very nature of the business requires 24 hour service. When only manual methods were employed, employees had to work overtime just to get orders out for the next day. The

SDA system enables the company to eliminate its overtime costs and meet its customer demands.

SDA is not restricted to state-side organisations. In England, Shell-Mex & B.P., Ltd. made a study in which it found out that 85 per cent of its customers' orders came in by telephone. This in turn generated annual workloads of three million sales tickets, five million punched cards, and a quarter-of-a-million invoices!

To expedite the processing of this paperwork monster, a special electro-mechanical device was designed. It consists of a very large console containing hundreds of buttons, each having on it the name and address of a customer. Near the console is a panel for product input data. A clerk wearing earphones sits in front o the console. He takes a call. presses a button for the name and address of the customer, and then, at the most, presses another four buttons on the panel to record quantity, brand, day of delivery, and packing code. This action is recorded on paper tape for later processing.

Interchange of SDA Information

One of the most interesting aspects of SDA is the growing trend toward interchange of information between private industry and government. For example, the State of California encourages employers to file their wage records on magnetic tape for input into the state large-scale computer system. These records are then used in conjunction with other SDA-generated records, such as those mentioned earlier, *Data Processing* describes this trend in a recent article: Almost 30 large companies are now shipping a single reel of magnetic tape in place of hundreds of paper sheets to the Social Security Administration record-keeping headquarters each quarter. These firms use electronic data processing equipment to prepare payrolls, and the tape is a by-product.

Five major components usually make up an SDA system: SDA machines themselves, communications, data processing, and information retrieval equipment, and display devices.

No single piece of equipment stands alone. Together they make up an effective SDA system. Several characteristics of SDA machines are:

1. They are low in cost relative to more elaborate computer systems.
2. Because what they do and how they do it is generally easy to understand, little operator training is needed.
3. Basically, much of SDA hardware is nothing more than adaptions and modifications of office machines which have been around for years, including electric typewriters, adding machines, calculators, and accounting machines. These basic machines now have the ability to accept and produce input/output media as paper tape, edge-punched cards, and magnetic cards.

However, although these older machines play a very important part in SDA, the trend today shows a move toward newer and more dynamic methods. MICR, or Magnetic Ink Character Recognition as an SDA tool has proved to be very successful in banks where MICR numbers imprinted on checks are used to sort out checks to pertinent accounts.

Perhaps the technique offering the most to SDA's further growth is OCR—Optical Character Recognition. Although the Bureau of the Census was highly successful in developing a specially designed machines, FOSDIC, to optically scan data for the 1960 national census, progress in other areas of government has been slow, as it has also been in private industry. But it's only a matter of time before optical scanning techniques will greatly improve.

DATA HANDLING

It is noteworthy that time and space are rapidly disappearing as barriers to the flow of business information. With the tools now available the question-answer-decision-reaction cycle, requiring the flow of data within the through the strata of a business organisation, can be about as fast as management wants it to be, even though the organisation components may be scattered throughout the world. Two of the tools which make this possible are data transmission and electronic data processing. Although data transmission predates electronic data processing by more than a hundred years, the blending of the two technologies is a relatively new art; a demanding one with few practicing specialists. Each of the various aspects of an information gathering, processing and transmission system—hardware, software, communication channels, forms, etc.—has its share of specialists. But the man knowledgeable in all phases of the blended technologies is still a rare individual.

Because the knowledge about telecommunications is "decentralised," the putting together of an information system generally requires a meeting of many minds. Technical minds must determine if what should be done can be done. Management decision-makers must decide if what can be done will be sufficiently effective to warrant the cost and effort involved.

Further complicating the picture is the virtually limitless choice of input/output equipment (terminal devices) available to the user. Devices most commonly used are those which handle perforated tape, punched cards or magnetic tape. But, computers are "talking to each other" in increasing numbers—nearly all third generation machines have this capability. Display/keyboard terminals, in which data appears on a TV-like screen, are becoming more common. Facsimile transmission is winning acceptance, although devices for this purpose are not numerous. Xerox Stewart Warner and Alden Electronics are in the market now.

Of course, all these devices require channels and converters, the basic ingredients of a communications link-up. Transmission channels most often used are either wire, microwave, or coaxial cable. Channels and converters usually are supplied by "common carriers" such as AT&T and Western Union. Service also is provided by General Telephone and Electronics and other "independents." The variety of the equipment and "grades" of channels available make it possible for a user to design two or three systems which will "do the job." How to choose which is best? The Bell System attempts to provide help in this direction by conducting seminars on a continual basis for top management and technicians form diverse industries. The criteria which Bell suggests as the basis for decision involve seven main factors: *Function* (what is the system supposed to do?), *distribution* (is the information coming from and/or going to multiple locations?), *volume* (are the messages long, short or both?), *urgency* (is the data needed immediately, within an hour, within a day, beyond 24 hours?), *language* (is the data in written form, spoken, graphic, in punched tape, punched cards or on magnetic tape?), *accuracy* (how critical is it that the data be error free? Would it be possible for example, to "read" a message if one word were misspelled?), *cost* (dependent upon all the cther criteria and to be weighed in terms of benefits).

While all the criteria are interrelated, and a change in one most likely would require a change in others, speed and volume probably are the two which will provide the initial clue to system configuration, at least to channel requirements.

Channels can be "shared," used exclusively, used in a dual mode (to transmit and receive consecutively or concurrently), used for both voice and data, or for voice, data and facsimile—there are numerous possibilities and the price varies. So, too, does the price of the input/output hardware.

Another cost factor is the labour required to operate the hardware involved in the system, particularly the hardware involved in collecting data and converting it to machine language. And, the cost of the exchange media—paper tape, magnetic tape, film, paper—should not be overlooked.

One system employing different types of terminals and channels is that used by the United California Bank, which has more than 190 branches throughout California.

A satellite data center in San Francisco is linked via two high speed IBM 7711 data communications units and a 24-circuit channel to the larger data center in Los Angeles. The satellite center is equipped with two IBM 1460 data processing systems and Model 1419 magnetic character readers for capturing data from MICR (Magnetic Ink Character Recognition) encoded checks. The data center in Los Angeles has a 7074 computer.

DOCUMENT STORAGE AND RETRIEVAL

[The] duality of knowledge has grown increasingly emphatic. In two centuries the store of information recorded about this world, its inhabitants and history has time and again doubled and redoubled. Since man's capacity to retain information within his own mind has shown little concommitant growth, the importance of knowledge of the second kind—of sources of information—has increased disproportionately. Fortunately, people have been bale to devise methods to supplement the ability of the individual human being to learn and remember where information is stored. Libraries and information centers, through the publication of reference works and indexes to their collections, immensely extended this ability, enabling the fruits of the pursuits of knowledge to be widely shared. However, in the familiar irony of success, discovery pyramided upon published discovery, until the flood of new information threatened in many cases to engulf the very institutions that provided the means for storing and retrieving it.

As the means for referencing current documents fell behind, the burden on the individual for locating and retrieving his own sources of information grew heavier. It became increasingly apparent that the technology that produced the information explosion would have to produce the means to effectively utilise it. First to nominate the computer as a candidate of the central library job of storage and retrieval was Dr. Vannevar Bush, himself nor a librarian but a renowned scientist, one time dean of engineering at MIT, head of the wartime office of Scientific Research and Development and advisor to the President on the establishment of government policy for the public dissemination of scientific information.

"There is increased evidence that we are being bogged down today as specialisation extends," he wrote in the July 1945 issue of the *Atlantic Monthly*. "The investigator is staggered by the findings and conclusions of thousands of other workers—conclusions which he cannot find time to grasp, much less remember, as they appear. Yet specialisation becomes increasingly necessary for progress, and the effort to bridge between disciplines is correspondingly superficial." His judgment of contemporary documentation procedures was that "professionally, our methods of transmitting and reviewing the results of research are generations old and by now totally inadequate for their purposes."

The Idea-Tracing Machine

Small and unreliable as it was in 1945, the electronic

computer, in combination with microfilm and display devices, was seen as an important key to a more effective means of sharing knowledge in the future. Projecting from known technology, Bush foretold the development of an idea-tracing machine—memex, he christened it—from which future generations could rapidly retrieve all the ideas, opinions and findings recorded by previous thinkers on any particular subject. By the early 1950s, scientists and engineers by the hundreds had set to work on projects to improve the new computer. They succeeded in making it reliable, expanding its memory and learning to programme it, and they made enthusiastic predictions about its shortly replacing human labour. And the new computers (named Mark I at Harvard, ENIAC at the University of Pennylvania, 604 at IBM UNIVAC I at Remington Rand, and Whirlwind I at MIT) lost little time in demonstrating to the world their remarkable speed at performing complex computations and data processing operations. In the field of information sciences, these early days are remembered as "the period of high enchantment." Disillusionment followed upon the discovery that practical systems for mechanical translation or fact retrieval were not to be achieved as easily as originally supposed. Once the troublesome hardware problems were solved, so that electronic malfunctions ceased to be a distraction, the enormous complexities of language and ideas stood exposed as never before.

Teach a computer to analyse natural language? Never had the need for linguistic research presented it demands so urgently as when the gap between potential and immediately realisable computer usage revealed the inadequacies in theory, comparative studies and experimentation with language. Researchers experimenting with the construction of artificial intelligence systems were awestruck at the enormity of their chosen task. Would-be builders of translating machines endured the agonies reserved previously for poets. And hopeful documentalist discovered that replacing the human librarian was to be no simple matter.

The computer as a library employee seemed at first capable of nothing more demanding than the simplest of clerical task: preparing lists of holdings, keeping circulation statistics, and the like. But even while computers were maturing mechanically, while researchers were learning to overcome the early programming limitations and linguistic and mathematicians were working on the theoretical aspects of communication, the information explosion showed no signs of expending itself.

Diverse as the fields of application may be, the principles of documentation system design are essentially identical, whether the orientation of the collection is toward physics or medicine, law or economics and whether the documents take the form of bound books, single pages, drawings or microfiche cards. Likelwise, the system functions are parallel in almost all respects.

Whatever the content or form of the documents, the organisation responsible for providing information about them must collect them, analyse and represent their content in condensed form, classify, index, catalog and announce them, and make the documents available with due speed, economy and convenience to the people who need them.

Similarly parallel is the recognition in many fields of the investment of intellect, time and economic resources required to bring the promise of fully automated information retrieval to fruition. Nevertheless, while information scientists continue to research and develop more versatile computer hardware, more sophisticated programming languages and better methods of system design, an increasing number of organisations are putting the best of modern technology to work now.

To explore the potentials for information transfer which the new technology is thrusting open requires a closer look at the workings, the problems and the technological interfaces of document retrieval systems. The subsequent discussion attempts to put these matters into finer focus.

Truth in Labeling

If one probes somewhat into the intellectual underpinnings of document retrieval he finds that almost all systems—from the simplest to the most complex—are based upon the concept of the condensed representation, or label, which describes in short form the essential contents of a document. The condensed representation is the primary device for relating an individual's interest to a set of one or more documents in a collection.

Conventional libraries, for example, employ such condensed representations as subject headings, Dewey Decimal or Library of Congress classification numbers, book titles and abstracts to represent essential content. By referring to these devices, library patrons are able to select items which pertain to their interests. Traditional representations have served the needs of libraries well in the past and continue to be adequate and economical for small diversified collections.

Fro large general libraries and special libraries with sizable holdings in specific areas, electronic data processing equipment introduces the possibility of devising new forms of representation more suitable to machine processing. The problem is to make them as useful as traditional forms.

- How *does* one describe what a document is about?
- How can the representations be made so concise that descriptions of the entire collection can fit in a

computer and yet be sufficiently informative for the user to judge whether or not a particular item pertains to his interest?

- Can a computer be programmed to read and represent a document automatically?

Questions of this nature stimulated considerable thought among the first generation of information specialists, and they devised numerous experiments to test the new ideas.

Several lines of research emerged from this activity. Some attempted to simulate traditional representations, such as abstracts, by means of computers. Other projects investigated new kinds of representations, such as term diagrams and ideographs—devices for "mapping" word and concept relationships. Most fruitful of the developments to date, in the sense of producing immediately applicable results, have dealt with techniques for indexing.

The index to a collection of documents is designated by today's information scientists variously as the "rime and central component in any information retrieval system," the "very heart of document retrieval," the "essential key to the document collection." It is the element that provides a common ground for a meeting of the minds of author, indexer and searcher—a meeting that necessarily precedes information transfer. Automation of the indexing process consequently merits consideration in some detail.

The indexing problem, from the point of view of indexer, searcher and designer of the indexing scheme, is essentially a problem of logic. How does the indexer describe the contents of a document; how does the searcher specify what he is looking for; how does the designer of the indexing language decide in advance how future users will state their information needs? Certainly such questions are not without precedent.

As an activity associated with collecting documents, indexing is at least as old as the Great Library of Alexandria. Nor has the aim of indexing—to make a large body of facts as accessible to people as are their own memories—changed significantly in many centuries, although techniques have undergone a continuous, if gradual, evolution.

The influence of the computer has resulted primarily in the search for new ideas in indexing and the formulation of new techniques which take advantage of the computer's speed and accuracy. The problem that technology is asked to solve can be illustrated by reference to common experience. Most people have tried their hand at constructing and using an indexing language. Anyone who saves records of any kind—letters, receipts photographs, recipes—has had to devise a scheme for tiling them if he hopes to be able to retrieve them conveniently at a later time.

Any document has an almost unlimited number of attributes by which it might be described. Deciding which are the most relevant to future needs requires first of all some prior knowledge about the circumstances under which the document is likely to be used, and then the construction of a logical bridge between the act of indexing and the act of searching.

The Language of the Index

The vocabulary of index provides the bridge building elements. Libraries and information centers today employ three types of indexing languages: classification, subject headings and key term vocabularies controlled by special thesauri.

Idea Classification

The problem of dividing all the territory of knowledge

into interrelated fields or categories of knowledge is one with which philosophers have wrestled for over two millennia. Indeed, classification schemes propounded by Aristotle in the 4th century B.C. have outlasted all the other schemes that ever were and are ever likely to be. The influence of his "categories" can still be seen in major classification schemes adopted today.

The classification of ideas provided an early framework not only for philosophical thought, but also for organising collections of documents—stone tablets, scrolls, books, etc.—by category subject matter. Through recent centuries, as human endeavour kept adding to the store of documents and to the depth and detail of information it became necessary to describe ever-finer subdivisions of the categories. Sometimes it made better sense to begin again with a whole new order, and two systems that did—the Dewey Decimal and the Library of Congress classifications—greatly improved the organisation and indexing practices of the nation's public libraries.

A detailed and comprehensive classification scheme, in itself a beautiful monument of logic, could be embroidered upon and refined indefinitely. However, as the orders of indentation increase, the system as a language for the retrieval of ideas beings to "break down" or lose its usefulness. The problem with using classification exclusively to index by is, of course, that few documents fit whole and intact into very narrow categories.

This creates a dilemma first for the indexer, who must decide to which classification category the document belongs. He can only hope that the potential user of the document will think to look for it in the "right" category. And the user, trying to outguess the indexer, confronts an even greater problem.

Subject Headings

Subject headings differ from classification schemes in being mutually exclusive. Whereas classification terms are related in a hierarchial scheme, subject headings are — or are usually intended to be — uniform in depth. All conventional libraries index their books by subject headings, a fact that attests to the viability of this concept. Nevertheless, subject headings exhibit the same major disadvantage as classification schemes—namely, the ambiguity inherent in the assignment of items to unique categories.

To compensate for this shortcoming and to make it easier for patrons to locate the information they desire, libraries have developed elaborate cross-reference systems. Ideas that are commonly associated are brought together by multiple catalog cards or "see also" references. The latter provide the searcher with clues as to where else in the card file he might find information pertinent to his interests.

Again, though, as the size of the collection increases within any subject area, headings have to be more specific, duplications proliferate, and the system grows cumbersome and annoying to use. Ractical difficulties, particularly in the retrieval of highly specialised technical literature, led to the search for new and more flexible methods of indexing.

The first truly innovative ideas of the century were advanced in the early 1950s. Competitive with each other as well as with traditional methods, they aroused an early controversy which has still not entirely subsided. The hottest winds revolved about systems featuring uniterms, descriptors and key words in context—and about their principal authors and proponents: respectively, Mortimer Taube, Calvin Mooers and Hans Peter Luhn.

Key Term Vocabularies

If any one characteristic distinguishes the unconventional systems from those use by traditional libraries, it is probably the matter of focus. Traditional methods fit incoming documents into preconceived categories (derived, to be sure, from centuries of experience with books and the various subjects around which they are customarily organised). Systems based upon uniterms, descriptors, key words or their relatives take as their starting point the information in a document itself. The information content of the document suggests the appropriate vocabulary—or key terminology—by which it is indexed.

The uniterm concept grew out of research by Dr. Taube and his associates at Documentation Incorporated to develop a method for indexing the heterogeneous collection of the Defense Documentation Center. The essence of their technique, which they called the Uniterm System of Co-ordinate Indexing, consists of analysing a document to select as indexing terms those words that best represent the content of the document. Depending upon the depth of indexing required, an average document might be assigned as few as two or three uniterms or as many as twenty or more. Each term by which a document is indexed provides an access point to the information the document contains. Conversely, each uniterm in the system provides access to all documents indexed by that term.

To retrieve information, one searches for documents indexed by the combination of terms representing the content of the information desired. Thus a document on the subject of "management information" would be located by coordinating the terms "management" and "information." The searcher might expect a document whose accession number was filed under both terms to deal with the coordinated subject of "management information." (The fact that it might also indicated a document on "information management" is a shortcoming of the original uniterm system which several modified versions get around by "pre-coordinating" terms likely to produce ambiguities). In addition to providing flexibility and multiple access to information, systems based on uniterms claim the advantage of a certain economy of operation. If indexing terms are lifted directly from the text of a document, people without extensive library training can be employed as indexers.

Systems based upon descriptors require more analytical indexing, but claim the advantage of a smaller, more easily controllable vocabulary. Descriptors are broader terms, descriptive of particular fields; they are derived by analysing a collection of related documents to determine the set of key terms sufficient to cover the field. As in uniterm indexing, multiple access to a document is provided by assigning to it all the descriptors related to its information content.

Control in both systems is achieved by constructing a system thesaurus—or list of all terms used to index the collection together with their synonyms. The thesaurus serves to relate terms of near similarity and standardises the indexing vocabulary.

As originally developed, both systems were operated manually. In the case of uniterms, for example, coordination referred to actual physical coördination of document numbers entered on matching columns of different vocabulary cards. Even so, the wide adoption of key terms systems was due to the fact that they were obviously suited for automation. The search and compare operation can be performed very rapidly by the computer. Given a list of index terms of computer can locate and print out in a few seconds the titles, authors and other relevant bibliographic data on all documents indexed by those terms.

Many of the variations suggested to expand key term indexing utilised the computer to keep track of the additional information. A number of information scientists sought to increase the pertinency of key terms by appending to them indicators of semantic or syntactic relationships: *roles* to indicate which term was on the giving and which on the receiving end of the action; *links,* denoting sequence or conceptual relationships; *prefixes* to specify generic levels; and numerical *suffixes* to indicate the relative importance of the key term in representing the content of the document.

The Keyword-in-Context (KWIC) concept pioneered by the late Hans Peter Luhn attempts to make the computer go a step beyond search and retrieval.

His "auto-abstracting" programmes have the computer select, by statistical methods, the significant words in an article. The computer then prints out the sentences with the highest density of these words. The words surrounding the key words act as modifiers. Seeing the key words in the context of their use helps the user to judge whether or not the article will be of interest to him.

As developed by Luhn and subsequently by follow information specialists, the original KWIC ideas have found two divergent applications.

A number of researchers have continued to experiment with statistical methods of analysing the text of a document to determine its subject content. Their long term aim is to programme the computer to act as indexer. Underlying these techniques is the assumption that the author of a document, consciously or not, reveals the key concepts in his paper simply by naming them an above-average number of times. If it were possible to develop a model of expected use frequency of all terms, the computer could count the actual word frequencies in any particular document, compare results with the model, statistically analyse the apparent differences, and with this data compute the document's proper indexing terms.

Statistical techniques have already achieved partial success toward this goal in cases where the experimental collection of documents was limited to a narrow range of subject matter. Whether or not the techniques are extendable to broad-based collections is still a moot question. Meanwhile, however, techniques growing out of experiments in machine analysis of natural text have made computer aided human indexing a present reality.

The second application of KWIC techniques emphasises the rapid listing capability of the computer. What are generally referred to as KWIC indexes are simply lists of document title terms (no ands, ifs, therefores, etc.) KWIC indexing works on the premise that a document title is a good indicator of document content. In the case of scientific articles, this premise is generally true, and KWIC techniques are widely used to construct fast and "quick and dirty" guides to technical reports and current periodical literature.

A Great Library at Your Fingertips

Of all the potential advantages of storing information from and about documents in machine-readable form, one that will have particularly striking impact on information gathering customs of the future is the potential of someday placing the contents of the greatest libraries in the world at the fingertips of people in their own offices or homes. While full realisation of this dream still lies a considerable way into the future, prospect for man-machine communication making bibliographic reference files available to remote users has already arrived. Users of the pilot SDC ORBIT system and the INTREX project at MIT, for example, are able to search library files by teletype. Cooperative projects being planned or implemented by other libraries include capabilities for one searching the contents of the other libraries include capabilities for one searching the content of the other by remote computer query.

The technique which makes this mode of operation possible is called on-line or interactive computer use. On-line techniques enhance computer utilisation by enabling people to control their own programmes directly, at the time the computer is processing them. This mode differs substantially from off-line usage, in which a user, ordinarily a programmer, turns his programme over to a specialist to process on the computer, receiving at some later time the results of the computer processing. With on-line usage, the user sits at a terminal device of some kind, usually a teletype machine or a cathode ray tube scope, and tells the computer directly—by typed commands—what to do with the data stored in its memory.

In the case of a document retrieval system, as developed at the present time, the user can formulate his search request at the teletype machine, specifying documents with a given list of characteristic—index terms, dates, subject areas, etc.—and receive a list of all documents in the collection that match the given description. Not only does such a system save the searcher time in going to the library and searching the card catalog, but it gives him information above and beyond what he would get from the catalog, thereby enabling him to make his search for more specific. The favourable results being reported about pilot man-machine systems lead to the expectation that opportunities for more people to deal directly with machines will expand rapidly. This expectation is further enhanced by recent progress in overcoming the two outstanding disproportions in the man-machine working partnership: the mismatches of speed-cost and of language. To resolve these mismatches between machine and human abilities, programme developers have brought forth, respectively, time-sharing techniques and interactive languages. A time-sharing system allows many users to share virtually simultaneous access to a single large computer. In the bargain, they share the cost of operating it. Concurrently, newly developed interactive languages are bridging the language barrier. "User-oriented," the new languages allow the non-programmer to communicate with the computer in a limited but growing number of natural English phrases.

The Information Machines

At the equipment end of the documentation system, many other technological advances just appearing on the horizon promise to have significant effects on the ease and pleasure and economy of retrieving information from future systems. For one thing, the practice of borrowing and lending is likely to decline as new copying machines continue to argument the quality and speed of reproduction, while simultaneously lowering its cost. Last year sales of copying machines topped $500 million. Increasingly, in industry, government, schools, wherever the same material has to be read by a number of people, the individuals are getting their own personal copies—markable, disposable or storable in personal files. If adequately protective copyright laws are worked out, copy machine manufacturers predict that books will be sold in vending machines long before the end of the century.

A second factor that will help to bring that possibility about stems from recent success in the development of micro imagery techniques. (Although the idea of reducing photographs for storage and subsequently enlarging them for viewing dates back nearly a century, it took the information "explosion" of the twentieth century to give the idea solid business appeal). Today, with a size reduction of 48,000 to 1, the entire Bible has been encoded on a tow inch square of plastic. The reduction process is expensive at present, as are magnifying devices for viewing. But prototypes exist, and predictions that entire library collections will one day fit into the space of a small box no longer seem absurd. At the more manageable reduction proportion of 20 to 1, the present federal standard, an increasing number of documents are being stored on microfilm, with resultant economic advantages in reduced storage space, transportation costs and reproduction. (To copy a microfilm record of 20 pages costs a few pennies more than duplicating one standard pages of text, but significantly less than copying 20 paper pages).

The major producers of copying equipment are also expanding rapidly into the facsimile transmission business. In contrast to the projection of a major encyclopedia publisher who foresees a future in which every family owns a pocket-sized set of encyclopedias, the transmission-oriented companies are predicting a day when a single set of reference books will serve an entire community. In their view, standard telephones of the future will be equipped with screens; whenever a person desires reference information he will be able to dial the local information utility and quickly get a display of the appropriate pages from documents pertinent to his interests. If he wants a permanent record of any pages, he can switch the signal from the display screen to his home printer and have an adequate reproduction in a few seconds.

The mechanical equipment required for such a system is well within the present state of the art. In fact, optical scanners have already been built that, working on principles similar to those of the familiar TV camera, can transmit facsimiles of anything over telegraph and telephone lines.

Pacing factors in the progress toward feasible electronic

display systems are threefold: the availability of communications lines, the cost of microwave transmissions and the development of easy-to-use input/output equipment.

Within the next decade or two, laser pipelines and satellite rebroadcasting stations are expected to be well along the way toward solving the first two problems. And even now developers of consoles through which the human communicates directly "on-line" with the computer are adding rapidly to the range and flexibility of input/output devices. Available today are tele-typewriters that permit communication through the medium of typed symbols and cathode-ray screens using the medium of light. In the latter case, letters, numbers or line drawings can be displayed by the computer, changed, erased or redrawn by the human hand wielding a pen that emits light instead of ink. Under development in the laboratories are super models which add to present devices the capability to sense and display both sound and colour.

What potentials for the process of information transfer will be created by the new dimensions in hardware programming and systems techniques are still conjectural. The availability of advanced equipment and programming languages will not only make document storage and retrieval more feasible, but will help to create the pressures of demand which are the starting forces for implementation.

Focal Point: The Information User

In the total context, however, it is important to keep in mind the fact that acquiring the components and putting them together in an efficient configuration are two different matters. A collection of advanced components no more constitutes an advanced system than a set of strong inks forms a strong chain. At least one other necessary condition must be satisfied. As SDC's study team for the federal Committee on Scientific and Technical Information phrased this requirement: "The system must provide a *needed facility* for its users through which they can attain objectives that otherwise are attainable less economically, or with greater difficulty, or not at all."

The whole point of collecting documents in the first place is to make their contents available to some user or group of users at a future time. From a utilitarian standpoint, the collection is valuable only to the extent that the serves this purpose. Therefore system design efforts have to be directed toward satisfying the information needs of the future system users.

To get a better hold on what these needs really are, a comparatively new branch of research is focusing attention on "users studies." Through interviews, observations and theoretical analyses researchers are attempting to measure and relate such variables as the factors that influence user satisfaction with a library and to evaluate present methods for indexing and retrieving information.

To a certain extent, studies of how people use information overlap with investigations directed toward the fundamental nature of information transfer — or communication—through the medium of the written word.

Philosophical and semantic problems are no more absent from these fields of inquiry than from any others. Indeed, Dr. Carlos Cuadra of SDC, in the introduction to the *First Annual Review of Science and Technology,* observed that "There is not, truth to tell, even clear agreement on what the word 'information' itself means and particularly on whether it implies a creative act of the intellect or a commodity that can be embodied in documents, transported and exchanged.

"Distressing as this ambiguity and lack of agreement may be," he continues, "they need not and do not preclude a constructive review of topics of current interest to users, designers and students of information systems and services." Neither do ambiguous terminology and a certain amount of grouping for directions deter an increasing number of individuals of diverse professional background from joining forces in an interldisciplinary attack on the problems of documentation.

Applying to documentation science the concepts, methods and experimental findings of their own specialised fields are psychologists with theories on cognition, sociologists investigating patterns of communication, philosophers formulating theories of meaning, philologists and linguist analysing language, mathematicians developing models of information storage and retrieval, electronic engineers producing new devices for information transmission, computer engineers developing the hardware and programmers the software of data processing, librarians contributing their long experience in document handling systems, and system analysts and designers defining the goals and operations of information management. Their successful endeavours will hasten the day, foreseen by Dr. Bush, when lawyer, historian, chemist, physician and even private citizen can sit at his memex-type desk and construct trials of reasoning "through the enormous mass of the common record."

Each step toward this ultimate system, by lifting from us slightly the burden of having to discover for ourselves the documents which are the sources of knowledge, enables us to devote more time and mind power to the discovery of the knowledge *stored* in the documents comprising the common record of man.

DOCUMENTATION AND COMPUTER OUTPUT ALTERNATIVES

The earliest alphanumeric microfiche recorders were intended to replace line printers in applications requiring the timely production of voluminous printed reports from machine-readable data. Such impact printer replacement applications, remain the largest, and most straight-forward, market for COM. For the production of circulation lists, serials holdings lists, union catalogs, and other batch-processed reports from machine-readable library data bases, COM recorders are invariably faster, generally more versatile, and often more economical than impact printers.

Recording Speed

The most widely-used line printers are impact-type output devices featuring a printing chain consisting of characters represented on embossed metal slugs linked in an endless loop. The chain rotates horizontally at high speed. Paper and an inked ribbon move vertically between the chain and a bank of hammers equal in number to the available print positions. As characters on the chain rotate into their appropriate print positions, individual hammers are activated to impact the paper, thereby driving it against the embossed metal characters. Since several hammers are activated simultaneously, the device appears to print entire lines at one time, hence the name. Other line printers employ drums rather than printing chains. Basic line printer operation is well-described in a state-of-the-art review by Wieselman (1977). Despite recent interest and advances in alternative printing technologies, line printers remain the most widely-used paper output device.

The rated, or maximum speeds of line printers have increased over the years to the current high of approximately

2,000 lines per minute. Actual speeds depend on several factors, including the size of the printable character set, and may prove significantly lower than rated speeds. The popular IBM 1403/N3, for example, is rated at 1,500 lines per minute but actually prints about 1,100 when equipped with a sixty-four character chain. The effects of larger characters sets are discussed later in this section. Multiple copies are generally produced on four-or five-ply interleaved carbon form sets. For copies in excess of form set size, the print programme must be re-executed. Five-ply paper may reduce the number of re-executions required to produce the desired number of copies. Four-ply paper, however, is generally preferred for legibility although the fourth copy itself may be of questionable quality.

The combination of low actual printing speed and multiple copy production via carbon paper can result it excessively long printing times for reports intended for distribution to many use-points. A two-hundred page, computer-processed list of items in circulation, to be distributed to twenty use-points in a multi-branch academic library, will require five printer runs on four-ply paper. Using the IBM 1403/N3 line printer described above, each run would require twelve minutes of printing time, plus time for decollating, bursting, and binding of printed copies. Well over one hour would be required to complete the entire job. By way of contrast, COM recorder rated speeds range between 10,000 and 50,000 lines per minute. Although actual speeds vary with page lengths and the method of input preparation, throughput rates of 15,000 to 20,000 lines per minute are realistic for the faster recorders.

A Kodak KOM-80 or Bell and Howell 3700 COM recorder, for example, will convert circulation data on an appropriately-formatted magnetic tape to latent images of two hundred pages of human-readable information on microfilm or microfiche in less than two minutes. Allowing time for microfilm processing, diazo or vesicular duplication, and any additional output preparation—such as the insertion of microfilm into cartridges—an in-house COM recorder could produce a circulation list, ready for distribution to twenty use-points, within half an hour. Even more dramatic throughout improvements can be achieved with the COM recorder/processors described in the preceding section. With its greater speed, a single COM recorder like the KOM-80 offers output capacity equivalent to about a dozen line printers—without a twelve-fold increase in cost. COM recorder speeds greatly exceed the capabilities of the Xerox 1200 Computer Printing System, an electrostatic printer rated at 4,000 lines per minute, and compare favourably with the IBM 3800 and Honeywell Page Printing System, two non-impact paper-output devices with printing speeds in excess of 12,000 lines per minute. In replacing line printers with COM recorders, computing centers and service bureaus translate increased recording speed into cost savings which can, in turn, be passed on to libraries and other customers in the form of lower output charges.

Economy

Several libraries have reported substantial cost reductions in the conversion of line printer reports to COM. Anderson (1973) describes such an application at the lost Angeles Public Library, where a 22,000 page patron directory required twelve printer runs to produce seventy-one distribution copies. Conversion to COM saved 82,000 dollars in the first year with projected subsequent annual savings in the 100,000 dollar range. While few library applications are so large proportional savings have been reported by Simmons (1975), Stecher (1975), Buckle (1974), Spencer (1973), and Buckle and French (1971).

The several factors that influence the cost-effectiveness of COM applications have, however, seldom been clearly delineated. To set anticipated COM cost savings in perspective. The application requires twenty distribution copies of a 200 page report to be produced fifteen times monthly. The cost comparison assumes paper output prepared on four-ply carbon interleaved forms by an IBM 1403/N3 or equivalent line printer equipped with a sixty-four character print chain. The printer is operated by an institutional or commercial computing center or service bureau at a charge of fifty dollars per hour, including decollating and bursting of output. Four-ply paper is priced at thirty dollars per thousand sheets.

Leaving aside discussion of the appropriateness of the microformat and reduction, the analysis of COM costs assumes the use of a service bureau equipped with a minicomputer-controlled COM recorder capable of creating 24:1, sixty-three page microfiche from a library-supplied print-tape. The cost per frame is 2.5 cents. Partial fiche are billed at the rate for sixty-three frames. Duplicate distribution sets, each consisting of four vesicular fiche, are priced at one dollar per set ($.25 per fiche). A modest charge is include for the preparation of a print-tape on the library's host computer. While the recording costs given in this example are realistic, they are subject to considerable local variation and should not be taken as a measure against which libraries can validly compare the cost they incur for similar services. Some libraries may pay a higher per-frame charge for preparation of an original COM fiche but a lower price for duplicate fiche.

The intemisation of COM costs includes a charge for microfiche display equipment, lamp replacement, and related maintenance. The analysis assumes the purchase of twenty high-quality, desk-top microfiche readers at a price of 225 dollars each. The total purchase price of 4,500 dollars is conservatively amortised over a three-year useful equipment life.

In this example, COM's substantial cost advantage is a factor of report length, frequency of updating, and the number of required distribution points. *As a general rule, COM will offer a substantial savings over line printer output for long reports, updated frequently for distribution to many use-points.* Line printer costs exceed COM costs beyond three updates per month. The cost differential widens rapidly with increased update frequency. At five updates per month, COM offers a 30% cost reduction. At ten updates per month, the cost reduction potential increases to 47.2%. At thirty updates per month, COM reduces output costs by 58.3%. This example assumes that the two other determinants of cost-effectiveness—report length and number of distribution points—remain constant at 200 pages and twenty copies respectively.

Line printer costs exceed COM costs where the number of distribution points reaches four. As with update frequency, the cost differential widens rapidly as the number of distribution points increases. At five distribution points, COM offers a 33% cost reduction. Cost reduction potential increases to 45% at ten distribution points and 59% at thirty distribution points. As indicated above, it is assumed that report length and update frequency remain constant at 200 pages and twenty times per month respectively.

Assuming that the number of distribution points and update frequency remain constant at twenty use points and fifteen times per month, line printer costs exceed COM costs for reports longer than about fifty pages. The longer the report, the more the comparison favours COM. At eighty pages, COM offers only a 9.5% cost reduction. At 100 pages, the cost reduction potential is 32%. At 300 pages, COM reduces output costs by 60.7%.

Output Quality

From the added-value standpoint, COM offers the additional advantage of greatly improved output quality at a significant cost savings. As noted, the third or fourth copies of a carbon-interleaved form set are typically of fair to marginal quality and utility. All COM duplicates, however, are made directly from the master microform and are of uniform quality.

Printable Character Sets

As noted in the introduction to this section, COM recording offers line printer users the advantage of increased output versatility, especially typographic versatility. Most line printers are equipped with a standard print chain of about sixty-four characters, including the upper-case alphabet, numeric digits, and selected punctuation symbols. This standard printer character set may prove unacceptable for library catalogs and other applications requiring the recording of bibliographic data. *Books: A MARC Format* (Washington, D.C.: Library of Congress, 1970), defines a printable set of 175 characters. While extended print chains—the ALA print chain, for example—have been developed, any expansion of the printable character set necessarily results in a reduction in printing speed.

The IBM 1403/N3 line printer, rates at 1,100 lines per minute with a sixty character print chain, will print only about 560 lines per minute with a 120 character chain. The user must weigh the value of enhanced output appearance against this severe reduction in work throughput. Like line printers, all COM recorders will print the upper-case alphabet, numeric digits, and frequently-used punctuation symbols. The basic COM character set totals sixty to seventy characters. Most alphanumeric COM recorders offer an optional extended set of ninety to 128 characters, including the lower-case alphabet and additional special punctuation and mathematical symbols.

The 128 character set is generally considered the minimum required to produce library catalogs and similar bibliographic products intended for patron use. Spencer (1973) emphasises the importance of upper—and lower-case output in overcoming the reluctance of COM users in public and academic libraries. The basic characters set furnished with the Cal Comp 2100 Series COM recorders corresponds to the IBM sixty character PN print chain, but an optional extended set of 136 characters includes the upper and lower case alphabet, six diacritical marks, twenty-four special characters, and sixteen European characters.

There is a trend toward extended character sets in newer alphanumeric COM recorders. In some units—the 3M Beta COM 700H and 700S, for example—the extended character set is standard. The DatagraphiX 4550 and 4560 feature a standard set of 128 characters expandable to 160 and 190 characters respectively. By way of contrast, the older DatagraphiX 4360 could print only sixty-four characters.

Most COM recorder manufacturers will create one or more special symbols to customer order. Both the Library of Congress and the New York Public Library have worked with COM service bureaus to develop extended character sets containing special diacritical marks and other symbols essential to the recording of bibliographic data in a large research library. Malinconico (1976, 1977) provides an excellent discussion of the nature of these extended character sets. The ease with which special symbols can be created, as noted in Section Two, depends on the method of character generation employed in the recording process. Character set changes or additions in DatagraphiX alphanumeric COM recorders require modification or replacement of the character-forming matrix located in the neck of the Charactron™ CRT. Character set expansion in dot matrix recorders in necessarily limited by matrix size—the greater the number of available light points, the greater the character-forming capability. The Memorex 1603, with its five by seven dot matrix, will print only sixty-four characters. The Quantor 105, 3M Beta COM 700S, and Bell and Howell 3700 employ a larger six by nine or seven by ten matrix to produce extended character sets. Character set expansion in stroke-generation alphanumeric COM recorders, such as the Kodak KOM-80 or 3M EBR, is technically simple, requiring a hardware change consisting of a minor modification of character-generating circuitry. Graphic COM recorders, like the Information International FR-80 or Cal Com 1675, also create individual characters by stroke-generation from pre-stored definitions. The FR-80, for example, stores from 128 to 242 characters definitions. As in stroke-generation alphanumeric COM recorders, these character definitions are represented in hardware, but in graphic COM recorders, an essentially unlimited character set can be generated through software modification. The generation of characters through software is, however, much slower than hardware generation.

The 3M EBR will print fifteen Greek symbols useful in mathematical applications, but large research libraries and smaller specialised collections may require entire non-Roman alphabets. The Cal Comp 2100 and DatagraphiX 4500 Series COM recorders offer optional Japanese Katakana character sets Chart II. DatagraphiX also offers a Cyrillic character set and will create Charactron™ matrices, to customer order, for virtually any language. Com manufacturers doing business in Eastern Europe and the Middle East have produced recorders with Arabic and Farsi character sets.

As might be expected, the increased cost of the hardware and software required to develop the extended character sets essential to the printing of bibliographic data necessitates higher prices on the part of service bureaus equipped with such special COM recorders. Malinconico (1977) cites frame prices in the range 4.5 to 9.3 cents for extended character set work.

Note that, as described above, the extended print chain decreases line printer speed by a half and doubles printing cost. COM costs, however, increase in only a relatively minor area—the production of COM master fiche. The cost of print-tape preparation, fiche duplication, and display equipment remain unchanged. While, in Table 7.1, COM reduced output costs by 51/3% in an application requiring upper-case printing only. Greater savings would be realised with increases in report length, update frequency, the number of distribution points, or the size of the character set to be printed.

Type Face, Size, and Intensity

A primary goal in COM type face design is to preserve legibility, often through several generations of duplicates, while striving for compatibility with optical character recognition (OCR) equipment. While there is no standard COM type face, the National Micrographics Association (1976) recommends, and many COM manufacturers employ, the European Computer Manufacturers' Association's OCR-B Alphanumeric Character Set, which is also available in an IBM Selectric element for typing source documents. Other popular sans serif type faces include Gothic, used in the Bell and Howell 3700 and 3800 COM recorders, and the NMA Microfont, one of three type faces that are standard and interchangeable with the Information International FR-80 recorder. Where typographic quality is essential, the Information International COMp80, an enhanced version of the powerful FR-80 designed for rapid and economical photocomposition of lists subject to frequent change, will print the three COM type faces offered with the FR-80; additional Roman, Gothic, Italic, and utility type faces commonly used in technical publications; and over three hundred graphic arts type faces. COM and utility type faces are created by the minimum number of strokes necessary to shape individual characters.

Graphic arts type faces are painted as a series of vertical strokes. Recorder software permits the interchange of type faces within a single microimage. The use of graphic arts type faces, however, greatly reduces recording speed. While the simplest alphanumeric COM recorders, like their line printer counterparts, can print characters in only one size and intensity, the 3M Beta COM 700H will print the Times Roman type face in four intensities. The Bell and Howell 3700 and 3800 will record characters at fifteen per cent larger than regular size. Users of the Kodak KOM-80 can select regular, bold, italic, or italic bold characters. Graphic recorders again offer the greatest type size versatility. The Applicon AP75 Micrographic Plotter, for example, offers an optional hardware character generator that will print eight character sizes, from six to thirty-two points. The Information International COMp80 will print graphic arts characters in sixty-four sizes from four to thirty-two points. Through software, sizes can be varied within a microimage—an important feature that permits, for example, the printing of the main entry portion of catalog data in one size and the collation and tracings portion in a smaller size.

Page Formatting

As noted earlier, the most prevalent COM page format emulates an eleven by fourteen inch computer printout page consisting of sixty-four lines of up to 132 characters each. Certain COM recorders, however, permit modifications in this basic format. For greater information compaction, the number of lines per page can be increased to seventy-two by the Cal Comp 2100 Series COM recorders; to eight-six by the

Bell and Howell 3700; to eighty-eight by the Kodak KOM-85 and DatagraphiX 4500 Series recorders; or to 102 by the Kodak Komstar recorders. The number of characters per line can be increased to 160 by the Bell and Howell 3700 and DatagraphiX 4500 Series COM recorders. The Kodak KOM-85 will record 172 characters per line. When equipped with an optional five by seven matrix, the Kodak Komstar is capable of recording 207 characters per line. Alternatively, line lengths can be reduced to eighty characters, producing the equivalent of an 8.5 by 11 inch document image and increasing the number of images on a standard microfiche to ninety-eight (in seven rows and fourteen columns) at 24:1 effective reduction; 325 (in thirteen rows and twenty-five columns) at 42:1; and 420 (in fifteen rows and twenty-eight columns) at 84:1. At 24:1, the 8.5 by 11 inch imaginary document results in a COM microfiche format that is compatible with the NMA standard for source documents.

For 16mm roll microfilm applications, the 3M EBR has a variable frame advance that allows users to significantly increase information compaction by reducing the gap between frames. When imaginary eleven by fourteen inch documents are recorded at 24:1 effective reduction, the normal advance leaves a gap of 5.4mm between cine-mode frames and permits slightly less than two thousand microimages per one hundred foot roll. By reducing the gap to .6mm, for example, an additional eight hundred frames can be recorded. In the comic-mode, the width of frames can be reduced to accommodate catalog card images and other bibliographic data formatted in lines of less than 132 characters. This flexibility permits the expansion of library catalogs and other dynamic data bases without unduly increasing the number of rolls, cartridges, or cassettes the user must handle.

Within frames on roll microfilm, the 3M Beta COM

recorders provide a number of special page-formatting facilities including proportional spacing, underlining, overlining, subscripting, and superscripting. The extensive formatting software of the Information International COMp80 permits both fixed and proportional spacing, ragged or justified right margins, automatic centering, and columnar printing.

COM vs. Online Systems

In addition to functioning as a line printer replacement for the production of batch-processed, computer-generated reports, COM-represents a viable, economical alternative to on-line systems in library applications without real-time information requirements. Where the real-time requirement is modest, COM can be utilised as one information storage medium in an economical hybrid system that combines microform displays with CRT or printing terminals. Where real-time information is essential, COM can provide continued access to important data in the event of on-line system failure.

COM as an Online System Alternative

There is an obvious and direct relationship between the accuracy of information and its value. In transaction-oriented applications—such as library circulation control, acquisitions, and cataloging—the accuracy of information depends on its currency. In batch-oriented computer systems, data reflecting the occurrence of a given transaction is processed and reported some time after the transaction itself. In a batch-oriented computerised circulation system, for example, the machine-readable master circulation file is updated, and circulation lists printed, on a pre-determined schedule. In such systems, the currency of reported information depends on the frequency of file updates and report production. Because batch-processed reports cannot reflect transactions occurring in the intervals between file updates, a circulation list produced fifteen times per month can be used with greater confidence than one produced five times. Because of the relative slowness of line printers, computer centers and service bureaus may not be able to schedule and guarantee the frequent and timely production of the very long reports characteristic of many library applications. In some cases, sufficient printer time may not be available. Veaner (1974) has further noted that libraries have rarely been accorded priority status by the computer centers that serve them. Academic computer centers in particular may be uninterested in the relatively straightforward, output-oriented applications characteristic of library automation. Faced with the inability to obtain printers output on an acceptable schedule, libraries requiring access to computer-processed data that is no more than a specified number of hours old may turn to an on-line, real-time information system. In such a system, a machine-readable circulation or other data file is maintained on magnetic disk, drum, or other direct access storage device. Unlike off-line systems which batch transaction data for processing against a master file at pre-scheduled intervals, *real-time* systems post transactions to the master file as they occur. File updating is simultaneous with the event rather than occurring at some time later than the transactions it records. Using a remote display or printing terminal, the master file can be examined on demand with assurance that the information it contains reflect the most recent transactions.

While on-line, real time systems offer the advantage of currency, with its implied accuracy, they can be very expensive. Although prices are dropping steadily, disk and drum storage still cost more than the magnetic tape used for master files in batch-oriented systems. Actual storage costs will vary from one computer installation to another and depend heavily on local accounting practices. Malinconico (1977) suggests a charge of $10,000 per month for a files of two million bibliographic records maintained in direct-access storage. On-line access requires a terminal at every use point. Programming requirements for on-line, real-time systems are complex, with long development times. In many applications, printed reports are still required to provide information during times when the computer is down or otherwise unavailable. To minimise costs in applications where currency of information is important but access to up-to-the-minute information is not essential, COM can be used to produce batch-processed reports at more frequent intervals than would be possible with slower line printing equipment or other paper output devices. With their greater output speed, COM recorders can produce long reports several times daily, providing the user with information that is no more than a few hours old in the worst case. COM's demonstrable cost advantages, detailed above, permit significant increases in report production frequency without comparable increases in cost. Figure 7.11, above, indicates that, for approximately the same expenditure, the hypothetical 200-page circulation report could be distributed to twenty use-points thirty times per month on microfiche or twelve times per month in paper form. COM report production at half-day, or possibly more frequent intervals, would not approach the costs of an on-line, real-time system for an application of this size.

While many applications can be satisfied with information that is no more than one-half day old, on-line real-time systems may offer superior performance in fulfilling certain information management requirements. On-line, real-time access to a machine-readable library catalog, for example, provides the user with information about the most recently acquired and cataloged items. Batch-processed holdings lists, as noted above, cannot reflect items acquired and cataloged in the interval between report printings. Some libraries consider access to the most recent machine-readable records an essential feature of a computer-based catalog. In such cases, COM can interface with on-line, real-time access in an economical hybrid system.

As an example, the heart of such a hybrid system would consist of a COM-generated catalog reflecting the library's holdings at the time the catalog was printed. New items are added to a machine-readable disk or drum file as they are cataloged. At pre-determined intervals, these new items are batch-processed against a master catalog file on magnetic tape and a updated COM catalog produced, duplicated, and distributed. Cataloging information prepared in the interval between catalog updates is fully accessible on disk or drum via remote terminal. The user seeking information about a particular item would first consult the COM catalog. Failing to find it there, the disk or drum file would be consulted to determine whether the desired item had been acquired since the catalog was printed. Users seeking information about very recent imprints would circumvent the COM catalog and consult the new items file first. The system is more economical than a completely on-line system in two ways:

1. The required amount of expensive disk or drum storage is reduced. A minicomputer located in the library might be used for the on-line file of newly cataloged items, with batch-processing and COM catalog production occurring at a remote computer center or service bureau.
2. Because most information needs will be satisfied by consulting the COM catalog, fewer printing or display terminals will be required. Although prices have come down, terminals remain from five to upwards of twenty times more expensive than microfiche readers.

Such hybrid systems permit many variations. An entire

brief entry catalog might be maintained on-line with full bibliographic information available on COM-generated microfilm or microfiche. The brief entry catalog would require less disk or drum storage. Alternatively, an author/title catalog might be accessible on-line in its entirety with subject and classified catalogs printed via COM. Such an approach both reduces direct access storage requirements and eliminates the complex task of programming an on-line subject-access application.

Backup

On-line information systems are vulnerable to hardware malfunction. Such malfunction may occur at either the central processing facility or at the remote terminal site. Hardware malfunction typically results in the partial or complete unavailability of machine-readable files. In the case of library catalogs and other applications where the continued availability of information is essential to daily operation, COM can serve as a relatively inexpensive back-up information storage medium. COM can also serve a useful back-up function in applications where limitation on available disk or drum storage do not permit the continuous maintenance of large data bases on-line. Because silver halide microforms, when properly processed and stored, have archival potential, COM is an appropriate medium for the long-term preservation of information. Periodic recording of library data bases on microfilm, combined with off-site storage of COM masters, can form the basis of an effective, but inexpensive, protection programme for library catalogs and other vital operating records.

COM shares some of the limitations of microforms produced from source documents. A reader is required. Microimages cannot be annotated. User resistance may accompany the elimination of paper reports. As already indicated, COM is generally not cost-effective for short or infrequently updated reports with few distribution points. Likewise, reports that are divided into separate parts for the use of various individuals may be best retained in paper. Paper output is generally preferred in applications requiring frequent reference between two pages or the comparison of pages from two or more reports.

Microfiche Indexing

Information from alphabetically-arranged library catalogs, call number lists of items in circulation, and other sequentially-ordered microfiche reports can often be retrieved successfully without indexing. Many COM applications, however, require an index to associate desired data with its location in a particular microfiche frame. The most prevalent COM microfiche formats provide for an index as the last frame on a fiche, positioned in the lower right hand corner. Placement of the index frame in this position is essential in applications anticipating the use of automatic fiche retrieval and display equipment such as the Bruning Model 95 or Image Systems' CARD reader. As with microfiche titling, software is utilised to extract class numbers, authors, titles, or other user-specified index keys from each data frame and list them in the index with their associated microfiche grid coordinates, expressed as an alphabetic row designator and numeric column designator. The ease with which this is accomplished varies with the software package. Cal Comp's Microfiche Management System, for example, permits extraction of index data regardless of its specific location on a page.

Vendour-supplied indexing packages, while very versatile, are written for the straightforward applications encountered in most report production environments. As noted in Section Two, special indexing requirements must be programmes by the user. If more than one index frame is required, they customarily occupy the last few corner frames. The best COM software automatically provides for a variable number of index frames. Instead of, or in addition to, the corner index, there is an increasing trend toward the placement of index frames at the top of each fiche column. These column indexes may be identical with, or more detailed versions of, the corner index. The column index technique sacrifices a few data frames to facilitate retrieval by keeping the user in close proximity to an index.

Another increasingly popular technique provides for a randomly-recorded microfiche or microfilm data base—of catalog entries, for example—controlled by a master index on one or more separate fiche. Each index entry delivers a roll number and frame number or a fiche number and grid coordinates. If botn the data base and index are on fiche, a dual carrier reader can be used to facilitate rapid referral from one microform to the other. For data bases on 16mm microfilm with a fiche index, the COR 701 reader will accept a cartridge and a fiche simultaneously. The microfiche master index technique, with a non-cumulating microfiche data base of catalog entries, is used by MARCFICHE.

In addition to functioning as a viable alternative to line printers and on-line information systems, COM can interface with equipment for the economical production of paper reports. In addition, the development of computer-input-microfilm (CIM) technology offers potential for extending a wide range of data processing capabilities to COM-recorded information.

Printing/Publishing

Several options are available for libraries requiring multiple-cope full-size paper output from microform data bases. The DatagraphiX 7000 Microfilm Input Platemaker will project enlarged COM microimages onto nine by twelve inch Datalith silver emulsion plates suitable for off-set printing of up to five thousand copies. The DatagraphiX 7000 accepts 16mm or 35mm roll microfilm, in either cine or comic mode. Magnification ranges from 3X to 36X. The Information International 800 Projection Platemaker produces off-set masters from 16mm or 35mm microfilm in sizes ranging from 8.5 by 11 to 12 by 18 inches. The 800 automatically searches for specified frames using image count marks. The LogE COM Printer automatically makes electrostatic offset plates or paper copies from 35mm microfilm at enlargements of 7X to 20X. Maximum print size is twelve by eighteen inches. For COM applications requiring a few paper copies for annotation or other reasons, the Xerox 970 is a programmable enlarger/printer capable of producing single or multiple plain-paper copies from all or selected microimages on standard microfiche in several formst.

Computer-Input-Microfilm

Computer-input-microfilm (CIM) is a variant of optical character recognition. A CIM device scans, interprets, and translates human-readable information on microfilm to machine-readable digital data on magnetic tape or other media. Thus, CIM is conceptually the opposite of COM. The advantages of CIM, outlined by Harris (1977), are obvious. Tape, disk, and drum storage are expensive, Bulky, and vulnerable to deterioration over time. Microfilm is economical, compact, and, when properly processed, archivally stable. Information on microfilm offers the additional advantage of being human-readable, permitting the simultaneous creation of reports for reading and computer re-entry.

Although CIM technology is still developing, the advantages of microfilm over paper in optical character recognition systems have long been recognised. Compact microfilm is easier to handle than bulky paper. Input documents need not be of uniform size. The paper jams commonly experienced with high-speed paper-document feeders are eliminated. Microfilm character recognition is accomplished by transmitted light rather than the more powerful reflected light required in paper OCR systems. FOSDIC, one of the earliest CIM devices, has been used, in several versions, since 1953 at the United States Census Bureau. Its application is described by Volk (1969) and McPherson and Volk (1962).

Grafix I, a complex and powerful CIM system developed by Information International, represents the state-of-the-art today. System descriptions are presented by Fenaughty (1974), Griffith (1975), and Holland (1976). Using a unique combination of hardware and software, Grafix I will read microfilmed source documents or COM microimages created in a variety of fonts and formats, including hand printing. Character recognition is accomplished through a masking technique enhanced by a probability algorithm. Broken type faces and hand printing are recognised by feature extraction. Rejected characters are displayed, with context, at an operator terminal for key-entered correction. Although any 35 mm microfilm input can be accepted, best results are obviously obtained from high-quality COM microimages prepared by graphic recorders such as the Information International FR-80.

The first Grafix I was built for the United States Navy. The system has since been used in several library-related applications. For the DATUM Information Retrieval System, an automated legal data base developed at the University of Montreal, Grafix I converted 16,000 bi-lingual pages of printed Exchequer Court proceedings to machine-readable form. At the University of California at Irvine, the system has been used to encode Greek text. In an application described by Burford and Clark (1975), the Hydrologic Data Laboratory at the Agricultural Research Service in Beltsville, Maryland uses Grafix I for computer re-entry of data previously recorded on COM. A date-entry error rate of less than one per cent is reported. As might be expected, Grafix I is a multi-million dollar device. The currently high cost of CIM technology necessarily limits its application in library work.

7

New Technology for Library and Information Science

> "It is literally true that no man has ever used more than a small fragment of his brain power... Almost from birth we are continuously blocked by conflicts among internal factions. Each man grows up to resemble a pair of moose with horns locked in battle. He dies of a struggle which he wages with himself."
>
> **—Dr. Lawrence S. Kubie**

In the present chapter we intend to discuss the developments in new technology that could be of benefit to people doing research in the humanities field. As a framework for this it proposes to describe some of the projects currently being supported by the Research and Development Department of an international Library, and use these to illustrate some of the tends discernible, and to identify some of the problems that may be raised as the new technology becomes increasingly and more widely available and used.

Remote Access and Document Storage

First, we support two projects in this area. One, organised at a reputed regional polytechnic, is concerned with the investigation of access to material stored at a remote site. His present device consists of a microfiche storage and retrieval device which is accessed by the user sitting at a remote terminal entering keywords. The appropriate fiche is then scanned electronically, held in a buffer store, and displayed on the screen of the terminal. The user can move round the image on the screen by using a joy stick control. When fully developed, this device will permit users keyword access to centrally held microfiche stores of text, graphics, pictures or any combination thereof. This should be compared with current systems such as BLAISE, SDC and Lockheed Dialog that permit access to stores to text only, and in the examples given, bibliographic text. The executive's current storage medium is microfiche, but he is about to go to the USA on a study visit to investigate other storage media available, in particular videodiscs. Videodiscs will permit the encoding of large quantities of text and graphics and voice or sound.

> "It is literally true that no man has ever used more than a small fragment of his brain power...."

A second project in this area, organised by senior academics of the Department of Computing at the University College of a metropolis involves the investigation of facsimile transmission over packed-switched networks (PSS, ARPANET, EURONET). So far the project has developed techniques for the storage and retrieval of data in machine independent form; for sending messages with the text; and for archiving. Facsimile itself is not new, it has been in existence for a hundred years or so — the newness of Professor Kirstein's activities centres about the use of digital, rather than analogue machines. His future activities include further developments of his earlier results, plus the investigation of how word processing and facsimile transmission can be combined in the interests of economy.

Word processors are suitable for the manipulation of text, but not suitable for the transmission of graphics or exact images. Facsimile can, obviously, cope with both graphics and text, but only by treating the text as another form of graphic and hence developers would not be able to take advantage of the efficiency inherent in the enconding of characters.

It was also planned, at a suitable stage of development, that the heads of involved departments would investigate the inter-working of the two systems, to permit facsimile images to be obtained from microfiche or videodisc stores. The exact storage device used in these projects would vary according to what is the current best bet from the technological view point.

However, we have a glimpse at devices that will permit users to access stores of graphics and full text and will extend on-line access from mere bibliographic information to the information itself, and will permit the setting up of new types of data bases, hitherto technically unfeasible. One of the outstanding issues still to be resolved in this area is one of resolution; the quality of the image. Both these systems digitize the data by scanning either the document or the fiche. How good of picture is presented to the user depends essentially upon how many "lines to the inch" are scanned. Too thin a density will result in a coarse image. However, the greater the density of scanning, the more digitilised information is generated all of which needs to be transferred down the telephone line or stored.

Although there are techniques used to compress the digitalised data so it can be sent down the telephone line more quickly, or stored more efficiently, probably for each application, a compromise will have to be struck between the level of resolution required or which may be acceptable, and the associated costs of transmission or storage.

Interest in man-machine interactions is not new. There has been research going on into this at a fundamental level for some time funded by other bodies. However, interest has been awakened in this area probably by the introduction of Prestel, a system designed for the mass market that really is simple to use. This should be compared with the other information retrieval system available commercially today — e.g. BLAISE, Lockheed Dialog and SDC, some of which are going to be demonstrated by Mrs. Vickery later on this afternoon. The command languages and underlying concepts are rooted in 1960's developments and so do take rather a long time to learn how to use and have not really to be recommended for use by the casual user. This has lead to library professionals developing skills in the use of these systems so that they can do the search required on behalf of the user. The simple retrieval software with Prestel, based upon the presentation of a menu of alternative courses of action to the user, for him his choice by the depression of a key on a keypad, has stimulated an awareness in manufacturers and information providers of the benefits of simple-to-use systems.

One cannot deny the large economic force encouraging this stimulation. The attraction of sales to a mass market are obvious, and has fostered an awareness that systems must be easy to use and reliable for them to be taken up by the man in the street. This new feeling was very much in evidence at the recent Viewdata 80 conference. Big business has woken up to the advantages of so called user-friendly systems. Our excursions into this area are modest but will provide a useful service and bridging between the information systems we are familiar with today, and those of the future.

Dr. P.W. Williams of UMIST has received institutional support to undertake some work on the use of microcomputers to act as friendly interfaces between the user and the computerised information retrieval systems. Dr. Williams hopes to devise a programme for the microcomputer that will interprete the users' requirements to the computer and make the computers response more readily intelligible to the user. In addition he will be looking at how the microcomputer could cope with the translation of commands from one command language to another. As you will see from Mrs. Vickery's demonstration, different systems have their own way of doing things, and it would greatly simplify matters for the casual user, if he only had to learn one set of commands, the micro translating them into the form most appropriate for the system currently being accessed. In this Dr. Williams will be following closely the initiatives of Alan Negus who has been doing a lot of work recently for the EEC on common command sets.

Electronic Journal and Word Processing Projects

As we have mentioned earlier one of the leading researchers' interest in word processors, and how they may be used in association with facsimile transmission. We have recently awarded a grant to the National Reprographics Centre for Documentation (NRCD) to investigate the usages of word processors in a special library environment, as well as being used to produce reports and duplicate letters, etc., and the normal business uses of the machine. As well, they will be investigating how a word processor can be used to produce more than one version of a journal — one in a format suitable for normal printing, and another version in a format suitable for producing microfiche. Staff at NRCD will be investigating the information retrieval capabilities of the machines — their uses and limitations, and also how the devices can be interfaced with COM equipment and other forms of output. Another project under negotiation at the moment is concerned with the research into the electronic journal concept. We hope that this project will start this year and at present delicate negotiations are proceeding on a number of fronts. On the one hand, negotiations are underway to lease some software appropriate for the job, and on the other hand, the final details of the methodology for setting up and using such a journal are also being finalised.

A whole family of different aspects will be looked at, including different forms of input, changes to refereeing patterns, changes to the journal format and in the behaviour of people making use of the facility. We do not want to dwell too long on this since the situation is still fluid. However this project and the word processing project at NRCD are examples of projects for which the essential novelty is not particularly the technology, but the application of the technology to an environment for which it was not originally designed. These two projects also underline ways in which people may find that traditional ways of doing things are being, let us hope improved, by the introduction of technology.

The New Technology Group

Remarkably, parallel with the establishment of some of these projects, especially the remote access and document storage ones which have been running for quite some time, since 1975, the Research and Development Department felt the need to set up a special committee to investigate new technology and how it could be applied to library and information problems. The department had become aware that developments were taking place in somewhat esoteric research environments, and perhaps in other application areas, the results of which could directly benefit the library and information world, if they could be caught and trapped.

A forum was therefore established of scientists and

information professionals to bridge the gap. It looks at existing and emerging technology to see whether the technologies are developing in such a way that the needs of library and information are catered for — and suggests projects where this can be encouraged. It looks at developing existing new technology to see how it can be used to benefit existing or new services and it is also concerning itself with the idea that existing professional staff need some educating so that they can make use of the emergent new technology when it becomes available, and are discouraged from the more unfruitful areas. Two areas that the Group particularly singled out of the new technologies that should have an impact in the library and information communities in the near future are novel input technologies and novel forms of storage. The latter I have touched on earlier in the form of Dr. Barrett's interest in mass stores (microfiche and now videodiscs). We had a brief flirtation with holography last year, but it's future is unclear at present due to internal rearrangements at Plessey (who are doing the research in the UK) and the possibility that for some applications holography has been overtaken by events — the introduction of videodiscs. However, mass storage, the technical developments and the reduction in costs over time will have an impact on library and information work in the provision of media to permit the economic storage of full text and graphics. Novel input technology has two themes. On the one hand, some devices like the hand print input device, and voice input when available are attempts to overcome the lack of user-friendliness of keyboards which are fine for those who can type, but no little deterrent for those that cannot.

Advances here include a pair of devices, that allow users to print on paper overlaying a sensitive pad. The movements of the pen are used to recognise the characters being printed — and the code for the character can then be passed to the computer or wherever. To the computer the device behaves like an ordinary keyboard. There are other devices also, like the Microwriter, with five keys. Combinations of keys are depressed to form the desired characters. The combinations of keys have been selected so as to mimic the shape of the characters to provide a simple aid to memory.

Devices of this nature continue the theme of a trend towards more user-friendly systems. The other feature that new forms of input bring is of course the possibility of inputting material other than text. Tablets have been developed that permit the input of graphics drawn on the them which have found applications already in the computerisation of maps, etc. The British Library has been supporting, since the autumn of last year, a research project based at Cambridge University Library under Mr. A. Tucker to look at the integration of Chinese and Roman script in automated library catalogues. Roman scripts have traditionally been input into library catalogue systems using keyboards, and Chinese and non-Roman scripts coped with by the usage of romanisations and transliterations. The development of the Ideographic Encoder at the Faculty of Oriental Studies and Cable and Wireless (a commercial company) has enabled the input of Chinese in its ideographic form.

The device consists of a drum over which is laid a matrix of Chinese characters. To input a character, it is located by rotating the drum and positioning the curser over the character—being identified by its row and column co-ordinates. These can then be manipulated in the way analogous to the way a code could be for a Roman character. Developments in COM have resulted in devices that are capable of the right definition and resolution to display these characters at the size required.

These two developments paved the way for the Cambridge

project which includes the further development of the Encoder to cope with a full character set; the selection and arrangement of the characters at the drum to suit non-native Chinese speakers the development of all the necessary interfacing required to handle the character sets with input facilities for Chinese Telegraphic code and all the official romanisations; the solution of problems of sorting and filing the Chinese characters; and the integration of this project with developments in the standards areas and the construction of a library catalogue containing part of the record in Chinese and part in, say English. Another interest the New Technology Group had was to negotiate with the appropriate bodies some test bed facilities, to have available for usage with suitable projects. The negotiation of specialised computing facilities always takes time, and the proposer of a project requiring computing or other complex facilities may not easily have access to them.

So far these include batch, parallel processing and novel input testing facilities. Predictions of the impact of new technology on the user are always difficult since there is generally a time lag between the technical feasibility of an operation and it being adopted on a large scale, due to financial assessment and organisational changes that are required for their further implementation. Some tentative effects can be predicted, as having some impact in the near future.

The user will observe a trend towards multi-purpose and integrated technology. Multi-purpose editing, terminals, that will permit access to computers, to Prestel, and to other remote stores, that will have facilities for receiving traditional print-out and facsimiles. Perhaps with voice and other sound capabilities. This approach would favour the naive user, the person without the time or the inclination to ascertain which piece of technology to obtain to access specific information sources; the larger markets that would ensure would also favour the user allowing potential reduction in cost. The necessary equipment and telecommunication sub-structures are gradually being developed and will emerge in the light of needs and market forces. The trend towards cheaper storage will allow users to computerise and automate new or larger data bases. The changing economic will be such that in the future, the storage of full text will become an economic proposition should it be desired rather than merely the bibliographic surrogates common at present. These developments, together with improved input devices will enable people to consider the establishment of data bases of graphics and other non-textual material, hitherto decidedly uneconomic, except perhaps on microfiche.

Users' needs will increasingly come under consideration. The effect of market forces attempting to reach a wider audience outside the traditional market for computerised products, and economic forces causing users to consider very carefully the efficiency with which such devices are being used will result in an emphasis on fitting the device to the user rather than expecting the user to conform to the rigours of the machine. This change will greatly affect the ease with which users take up the new technology and greatly affect the new uses to which it can be put. These will favour the trend towards electronic dissemination of information and people feeling as happy to communicate via a terminal as perhaps they do by telephone today. The researchers in some organisations will find that his reports and papers are being prepared increasingly on word processor equipment. He will see the benefits in increased freedom to create, amend and change his work. The use of retrieval software, either in the word processor or in the computer to which copies of documents could be passed, can be used to enable the researcher to manage more efficiently reports created by him, or other colleagues. Increasingly, the user may find himself disseminating his research results via electronic means, benefiting from the speed that electronic communication can generate. The form of the journal article favoured by this medium and the type of communication may well differ from the traditional form. As far as those concerned with the humanities are concerned; perhaps the most important thing is a ready understanding of the needs of the group is essential, so as to be able to influence the evolution of the new technology to take account of the undoubted special needs of the humanities researcher and his information needs. Education of future users should be a serious consideration so that they can see the benefits (or otherwise) of the changing technology, can adjust to the changing scene, and accept the changing role of the information centre as more and more information becomes available.

The economic situation is changing rapidly too, so it is as well to keep this factor under consideration also so as to be able to determine at what point it is best to introduce technological change.

In fact, the need for facsimile transmission from remote access storage facilities was discussed. Its importance was questioned, when fiche can easily be transmitted by post. A central storage facility was seen as having the advantage of facilitating up-dating. It was stressed that decisions did not to be made between new technology and existing technology. There is a need for a mix and to select the technology most appropriate to the needs of a given situation. For instance, some fiche might be required on hand while some might be placed in remote storage. In the context of the use of technology to facilitate up-dating, it was suggested that there might be a need to freeze up-dating in order to obtain a snapshot view. There was some discussion of the drawbacks of facsimile transmission, particularly the time taken for scanning. It was suggested that the implementation of facsimile transmission would depend on the economic climate, which affects the balance between central and local storage. Developments in word processing and its applications to libraries were discussed.

The National Reprographic Centre for Documentation at Hatfield Polytechnic is evaluating the use of a Word Processor, not simply for preparing reports, but also in terms of exploiting the accompanying soft-ware supplied by the manufacturers, with particular reference to the capacity to take over traditional library functions. Concern was expressed about the long-term conservation aspects of new technology.

It was admitted that while information is available concerning microfiche, less is known about videodiscs, which are currently mainly used for entertainment purposes in the United States. Questions of copyright and security were raised. Not all the copyright issues have been resolved. It was questioned whether humanists are less willing than natural scientists to share there current thinking. It was pointed out that there are means of providing electronic locks for personal files. One of the problems of technology was seen to be that it is moving so rapidly that ideas may not be exploited commercially because they might be overtaken.

Generally, Librarians have often demonstrated a pre-recorded online search. The search dealt with the history of violent crime in the eighteenth century. A number of different data bases were used, on two systems, Blaise and Lockheed Information Services. The recording was done using the Mediatron, a device which enables real searches to be stored, together with voice-over and cued slides. The search was presented on a V.D.U. and a monitor.

As an example, the bibliography of a classic book, "The making of the English Working Class" by E.P. Thompson, published in 1965, was cited. Thompson lists papers found in the Public Record Office, in London, in the Manuscript Room at the British Museum and in the Sheffield Reference Library. He also consulted the Radcliffe papers at a private country mansion, at Rudding Park, Harrogate. It was pointed out that students engaged in work for a PhD need to look in depth at a narrow field and so inevitably need primary materials. Very few primary materials are recorded in machine-readable form, and the demonstration was concerned with improving access to secondary sources, in order that time thus freed could be devoted to teaching and thought.

The prerequisites for conducting an automated search are:

- a terminal
- a. V.D.U.
- a printer
- an outside telephone line
- a modem
- an intermediary who knows the command language of the system and the data base or the end-user with this knowledge.

The demonstration showed now different numbers of references could be obtained from different data bases, using the same search strategy. The benefits were obvious in terms of speed, but some drawbacks were pointed out. An amusing example was the finding of a reference on the murder of newspapers (the machine is not able to cope with metaphor).

The first part of the discussion was concerned with the relevance of searching in the manner demonstrated. In response to a question about whether the searching of data bases made sense to the users, Mrs. Vickery said that the historians who had been approached for the pre-recorded search had certainly felt so and were themselves using the technique to update a particular publication in writings on British history. Some assessment of the value of searching data bases in the sciences had already been done and the possibility of assessment of its use in the humanities was being considered. One issue discussed was whether the interest of humanists in searching data bases in machine-readable form would only develop when primary sources could be accessed in this way. Another matter for discussion was the place of the interview with users for whom a search was to be conducted.

The question was posed concerning whether the pattern of interviewing prior to search would continue and whether users would therefore continue not to do their own searching. It was suggested that the major problem in users conducting their own searches was that of the knowledge of different command languages. The situation would improved if command languages were standardised.

Another advantage of conducting interviews with the potential user is that this helps the user to specify his/her requirements. This could be particularly relevant to the cost of searching. The cost of searching was discussed. Searching is getting cheaper, but obviously the cost depends on the search. One issue is that of the value placed by researchers on their own time normally spent on searching. Another question raised was that of the possibility that the more effective the search, the more expensive the follow-up, for instance in terms of inter-library loans.

Aspects of the usefulness of searching data bases were mentioned, particularly the use of the technique to the researcher for finding new material. Comments were also made on the potential use of the technique for teaching purposes.

The Need for Resources Guides

Basically, the need for radically improving the available guidance to library and other research resources in the UK has been repeatedly stressed in professional literature and meetings for at least a decade and a half, and with increasing frequency. In 1965 the Library Association's report *Access to information* envisaged one function of a national bibliographic centre as 'compiling and publishing detailed guides to sources of information.' The present seminar's predecessor in 1975 felt that '... not enough was known about special collections of book and non-book materials in the humanities.... More research was wanted on the requirements of users of the various guides to literature and resources.' In the same year a seminar of the SCONUL Information Services group '... especially noted the need for improved guides to good collections of specialised material.' The most extensive study to date of resource guides and library directories, conducted in '1976 by Aslib on behalf of the British Library, pointed out that no coordination existed for identifying demand for resource guides, updating existing publications or planning new ones. A recent article of my own has been devoted to the question of how best to characterise libraries and collections for the purposes of entries in resource guides.

This sector seeks to focus this widespread concern over inadequate resource guiding on the three practical questions which will bear directly on any future initiative:

(a) What would be the advantages, if any, of developing coordination and planning procedures to be applied to the preparation of resources guides?

(b) What should be the qualities of a good resource guide, and what principles should underlie its preparation?

(c) What contribution can resource guides be expected to make towards facilitating study and research, especially in the humanities and social sciences?

What is the distinctive usefulness of a guide to library, archival or other research resources? If the enquirer is not using the guide to find an address or telephone number (which is the primary purpose of a library directory in the narrower sense), and if he is not using it to try to locate a specific publication (which is the primary function of a union catalogue) — then the resource guide's sole remaining distinctive feature is the description it gives of each collection. In other words, *subject access* is the only service which a resource guide can offer if it aims to be more than an address list. The enquirer *may* also use it as an aid in guessing where particular works are to be found, if he has no access to union or other catalogues, just as he *may* use it to find a name or telephone number but he is likely to expect, in the first instance, reliable information about the character of the collections included which will enable him to judge those most likely to aid his work.

A guide which can provide this kind of information will also possess the basis for other contributions to research: it can facilitate the planning of research so that it takes full account of all existing resources in the field; it can permit the identification of inadequate or non-existent resources in particular subjects or locations; it can provide the foundation for better cooperation between libraries; and it can give libraries better standards of comparison between themselves. If resource guides are to provide adequate subject access for the user, their compilers will need to differentiate between users and between subjects.

The distinction sometimes made between `general' and 'specialised' resource guides is not, in my view, a useful one. It suggests that the 'general' enquirer may find it easier to use a guide which describes collections only briefly, and which probably covers holdings in many subjects in a large number of libraries. The 'generalist' who will benefit more from such guides in a mythical being. If an enquirer turns to resource guides at all, he will — on the assumptions made earlier — be looking for libraries likely to hold material in the subject or topic which interests him, however limited his knowledge or qualifications in that subject may be. Lack of detail in a resource guide, combined with a multitude of entries, will yield either far too many 'possible' locations, or will be too unspecific for the user to identify any 'possibles' at all. This is not to say that two or more resource guides might not be designed to cover the same subject, or indeed the same libraries, if they were orientated towards people with different kinds of interest in them.

It might, for example, be appropriate to have one guide to resources in history for the undergraduate student, another for the amateur local history enthusiast, and a whole series for postgraduate and other advanced researchers. My point is that none of these is a 'generalist'" they all have specific and differing needs which should determine (a) which collections will concern them, (b) what range of material in those collections will need to be included in the guide, and (c) how the holdings should be described.

If, then, a resource guide is to be compiled primarily to facilitate access to collections by subject for defined classes of users, its preparation and presentation will need to observe several important principles. Firstly, the coverage of the guide will need to be carefully defined, whether it is of a traditional discipline, an 'area study,' or a developing interdisciplinary subject. The class of users will also need to be defined, contacted, and consulted at the planning stage of the guide.

The compilers will need to be familiar with the structure and terminology of the subjects to be covered, so that the collections can be described consistently in the terms, and to the degree of detail, which are most appropriate. Consistency and thoroughness in description are something which the user has a right to expect from a resource guide: that is, that all significant collections, throughout the range of topics which the guide purports to cover, should at least be mentioned in the entries for the libraries concerned, and should at least be indexed too. As noted above, the compilers will have to decide on the depth to which the collections will be described, and this will vary with the guide's subject and readership. For instance, should we note only the presence of holdings in 'Russian history,' or should we distinguish between collections on the economic, political, military and local history of Russia?

A decision on this will require the compilers to fix the terminology and the hierarchy of subject division to be used both in characterising the collections and in preparing the index. It needs to be remembered that the description of each collection will not be read in isolation: it will be compared with other entries in the guide. Not only must all relevant holdings be mentioned, but all the 'mentions' must use a carefully-controlled vocabulary and variation of length, to ensure that — for example — a 200-title special collection in a small library is not described with a much greater verbal fanfare than a 2000-title holding on the same topic in the Bodleian. An important practical consequence of this requirement concerns the process of gathering information for the entries in the guide. Whatever combination of questionnaires, personal inspection and literature searching is used to elicit the necessary data, it is essential that all the collections should be reported on in the terms set by the compilers. Faced with an unspecific enquiry about their holdings, no two libraries will (left to themselves) respond with exactly comparable accounts.

Enquiries will need to be persistent enough to verify exactly what every library has in the subject of interest, rather than simply hoping that all of them will possess staff with enough time, knowledge, records and inclination to supply the details required. A question which will have to be resolved separately for each guide is whether, and if so to what extent, the descriptions of collections should mention individual works or items. We suggested above that resource guides can offer a contribution to research which is distinct from that offered by catalogues of books or lists of periodicals. A resource guide can (or should be able to) provide information on the subject profile of collections which catalogues and title lists cannot give because of their itemised nature and, usually, their author/title arrangement. There is the further consideration that resource guides which note the presence of some individual titles will run the risk of misleading either by the omission of some locations or by the undue prominence given by haphazard occasional mentions.

There may be some merit in recording fully the location of a limited number of 'key' titles, or (in a subject where the volume of data is not impracticably large) in incorporating, say, a union list of serials into the guide itself.

In fact, there is no lack of 'resource guides,' 'library directories' and 'guides to sources of information.' Nevertheless, the opinions quoted in the introduction to this paper emphasise that there are still many subjects and specialities which are not served at all by such publications. Just as importantly, if the contentions of this paper are accepted, many of the compilations now in existence are far from being the thorough and consistent guides to available material which the enquirer has a right to expect. If, then, uncoordinated action by organisations and individuals has failed to provide adequate guiding to British research resources in many subjects, there may be a case for establishing some fresh organisational form which could identify subjects or areas for which resource guides (or better resource guides) were desirable, and could promote and advise on their preparation and publication. The concept of a point of responsibility, at national level, for facilitating access to library resources, has already been accepted in Canada and USA.

The National Library of Canada's Resources Survey Section, formerly the Office of Library Resources, has for some years been issuing the series *Research collections in Canadian libraries,* while the National Referral Center, attached to the Library of Congress, is producing the series *Directory of information resources in the United States.*

The functions of a similar agency in this country, as they related to resource guiding, a might be on the following lines:

1. Seeking specialist organisations and/or individuals capable of preparing suitable guides, and encouraging initiatives from such specialists.
2. Undertaking the necessary consultations and research in order to identify subjects or topics for which guides to research resources were desirable.
3. Responding to applications for limited grants to assist in the compilation of resource guides.
4. Giving or obtaining expert advice on any aspect of a guide's planning, compilation, design or publication.
5. Coordinating, though without any mandatory powers,

plans for the preparation of guides in adjacent or overlapping subjects.

6. Using the findings of resource guide compilers to assist it in providing the appropriate authorities, as well as researchers and librarians at large, with assessments of the quality and distribution of the country's research resources in specific fields; to formulate recommendations for improved coverage; and to indicate the scope for better cooperation and more efficient use of resources.
7. Assisting in the publication of resource guides of a high standard, either by establishing a resource guide series published by the office itself or its parent body, or through agreements with publishers elsewhere.

Obviously, it is important that any central office of this kind should not attempt to bring the actual compilation process of resource guides under the administration of its own staff; nor, in encouraging high quality, should it impose rigid conventions upon the guides approach and the presentation. The real services which a 'resources survey office' could perform in this respect would seem to lie principally in making better use of specialists' expertise and in promoting cooperation between specialists in order to provide resource guiding of a higher standard and in more fields. Building on this work, it could greatly improve the present state of our knowledge about provision for research in any country.

Generally, we want to look away from fully fledged historians, and PhD students back to the undergraduate level—at which researchers pick up their attitudes to librarians and information services and their approach to seeking information, and in particular to look at the work of the Travelling Workshops Experiment concerning user education for history students. We should also explain at the outset that the Travelling Workshops Experiment has now become part of a commercial undertaking known as Newcastle-upon-Tyne Polytechnic Products Limited—and that I was with the team for the last phase of the research project alone. We propose to introduce the Travelling Workshops Experiment history package to you now, discuss some of the thinking behind it, and then have a look at one of the components of the package—an introductory tape-slide programme which lasts for about 20 minutes.

To cite an example, three subject specialists were appointed to the research team at Newcastle to work in the areas of biology, social welfare and mechanical engineering — and hereforth we shall defer—and refer any enquiries on the early development of the Travelling Workshops Experiment to Colin Harris, who as many of you know, was one of the founding members of the team. For those who are interested a list of publications about the project is available and so is the British Library Research and Development report. Suffice it to say that the project went through several evolutionary stages, and with the team's experience in conducting formal workshops for undergraduates they moved to the adoption of a self-instructional approach in the preparation of learning materials.

For those who are not familiar with the Travelling Workshops Experiment, or with the idea of information learning packages we shall briefly outline ways in which the first three packages, developed by the Travelling Workshops Experiment, have been used:

1. The package has been used in workshops of some kind — typically conducted on two or three afternoons in successive weeks. Workshops generally incorporated an extensive display of sources.

2. The materials have been made available in the library itself over a period of time, from a week to a term — a method which avoids the artificial atmosphere of a workshop.
3. Entirely independent use of the materials by students has occurred, but, as you might expect, this was most successful where combined with formally time-tabled seminars.

To return to the history package — by the beginning of 1979 the Travelling Workshops Experiment had already received a second grant for the purpose of investigating whether the common framework of the first three packages was appropriate in other areas — particularly in the humanities, and history was the subject chosen.

We might remind you here of our predecessors who met at Gregynog where "warm agreement was expressed all round of the idea that young scholars and students, in general, needed a better training in information services than the average supervisor could give."

The plan, then, was to see how far the existing package framework was appropriate for the subject of history—and relevant to the needs of students of history.

In order to achieve this relevance and also to give the materials produced the full weight of academic authority, a new method of preparation was tried. There earlier packages had been developed solely by subject specialists who were also librarians, but this was a joint work. We sought to marry the bibliographical skills of myself as a trained librarian, and also a history graduate, with the critical authority of an academic consultant — Professor Norman McCord of Newcastle University. The Professor maintained a fairly heavy teaching commitment, and memories of my own student days were not altogether dim — so between us I feel we kept the question of relevance high on our priorities.

We were concerned to equip users of the package with the ability to evaluate the sources they meet. Naturally we endeavoured to give some critical comment on the major sources cited in the package but our hope is that as a result of using this package students will be in a far better position to assess the authority, currency and relevance of material which they encounter in future.

Notably, because treatment of this area is an integral and compulsory part of most undergraduate courses. Secondly, we felt this to be an area in which undergraduate have reasonable access to primary sources, and is therefore an area in which many students choose to pursue research for dissertations and projects, so common now in the requirements of a first degree. That the coverage spanned three centuries was to our advantage too in that it prevented us from becoming too narrow in selection of material and examples. Now to the components of the package. The main vehicle of instruction is the student handbook. Implicit in its structure, chapter by chapter, is a systematic search strategy.

It moves from the consultation of reference works, and books and bibliographies, looking at the use of theses, conference papers and so forth. Exercises, for which students are required to use particular sources, are included at the end of each section in order to suggest the range of material available. The final step, for some students, is the identification, location and use of primary source material. At each stage our intention was to outline the nature of the type of source (that is — what *is* a bibliography, and what *is* an abstract) and then to direct attention to major and standard items, and lastly to indicate the variety of material available through the inclusion of particular examples. We need not embark on a tedious recital of the content of the handbook but suggest that you might examine it carefully yourselves if you wish. Here we just want to bring to your attention one or two points.

Firstly, in selecting material to be included, we tried to describe only standard and essential tools and other sources were named purely as examples of the type of source under discussion. Much of the liveliest exchange between the Professor and me derived from this question of selection, and it is worth indicating that we occasionally felt obliged to include publications which we knew to be limited in usefulness. For instance we indicated that the *Annual bibliography of British and Irish history* is the most up to date of current serial bibliographies but that it is not annotated.

This example leads us to a second point - the importance we attached to introducing students to the wide range of 'one-off' subject bibliographies available to historians. We discussed the points students should consider about the compilation and content of a bibliography which they are using.

Further, a key problem was how much information should be included on primary sources. We examined these in groups: Documentary records, Archaeological evidence, Audio-visual materials and we had a nice *convenient* section on Miscellaneous sources, including oral history and place names. I hasten to add that the categorisation of sources used was definately pragmatic! Some introductory points on the problems of using primary sources precede a discussion of the different types of record. There is no attempt to give comprehensive coverage but rather to indicate useful sources of information.

A belief section of access to records rounds off the chapter, by indicating repositories such as the P.R.O. However, I must emphasise that although we identified major repositories, and indicated the wide range of smaller collections, we were anxious to extend a restraining hand to avoid over-enthusiastic sorties of valuable resources. The posters displayed given a general indication of the range of reference books available, and the other two were designed as more specific instructional aids, which can be used as a method of point-of-use instruction in a library as well as being used for workshops and so forth.

For example, the poster explaining the use of the *Art and Humanities Citation Index* followed a format successfully used by the team with other citation indexes. A more detailed explanation of how to use this index is provided by the audio-cassette programme, which lasts for some 15 minutes, and can of course be used by an individual or with groups. The listener handles the different parts of the index while listening to the tape—not only learning *how* to use it, but also gaining some familiarity and confidence in handling the tool.

A teacher's manual is provided for the assistance of academics or librarians, or preferably both, who are planning to run a user education course based on the package. This manual grew out of the experience of the team in giving workshops, and so is very much a practical guide. Before we go on to show the tape-slide programme I'd like to look again at our main objective—which was to test the applicability of the established framework of the first three packages to this subject.

In fact we found that the established pattern was appropriate. Certainly it was essential to first consider the bibliographic structure of the subject—and then we made changes in emphasis finding that we did not need to make changes in the framework. In this package you find more extensive treatment of bibliographies, introduction to a wider range of abstracts and indexes, and of course an examination of primary source material. Greater emphasis is laid on the need to evaluate and assess material, and on how to go about this. The only real change in the presentation of material is the use of the enlarged typescript in this package—subsequent to criticism of the earlier packages.

Well—the package went on sale at the end of last year—and the Travelling Workshops Experiment has become part of a commercial undertaking know as Newcastle-upon-Tyne Polytechnic Products Limited. Naturally it is for time, and use, and package purchasers to say how successful this product is. A preliminary survey of those who have bought the package to date indicates a generally favourable reaction, particularly to the handbook. On the whole the more specific comments on content fit in with what one would expect—one person telt *Historical Abstracts* should be omitted, (since it is now on-line) another felt *Arts and Humanities Citation Index* was irrelevant. One felt the treatment of research methodology and primary sources to the pleasing, another that this is irrelevant to the need of undergraduates. A fair number were concerned that not all the sources cited are available in their library, and one or two points were raised about the tape-slide programme.

We want to draw together first some points about the preparation of these packages which might profit from further investigation.

1. There is certainly scope for research on the effectiveness of the use of different combinations of media, and the exploration of other forms, such as video.
2. The possibility of providing guidelines and aids to facilitate the inclusion of more 'local' aspects of library instruction by particular institutions should be considered. This need has certainly been articulated

by package users and could have the advantage of both tying in the package with local library provision, and relating it to work currently being undertaken by students.

3. The number of requests for full instruction and guidance on use of all the package has also been significant. This problem is perhaps greater in respect of this package than with the with the earlier ones which had been demonstrated by the team in workshops and at forums. Developments in this area might move in the direction of grouping together academics and lecturers who have used the package to share their experiences.
4. Further investigation of whether library instruction should be the province ot the lecturer or librarian—or a shared task—would be profitable. This is bearing in mind that where packages have been used by lecturers, in the past, user education programmes have been very successful and that the package provides bibliographical expertise which (dare I say) is not always at the fingertips of the historian.

8

Miscellaneous Issues

"Credit is like a looking glass, which when once sullied by breath, may be wiped clear again; but if once cracked can never be repaired."

I

INFORMATION ARCHITECTURE

The term information architecture describes a specialized skill set which relates to the interpretation of information and expression of distinctions between signs and systems of signs. It has some degree of origin in the library sciences. Many schools with library and information science departments teach information architecture. Information architecture (IA) is the art of expressing a model or concept of information used in activities that require explicit details of complex systems. Among these activities are library systems, Content Management Systems, web development, user interactions, database development, programming, technical writing, enterprise architecture, and critical system software design. Information architecture has somewhat different meanings in these different branches of IS or IT architecture. Most definitions have common qualities: a structural design of shared environments, methods of organizing and labeling websites, intranets, and online communities, and ways of bringing the principles of design and architecture to the digital landscape. Historically the term "information architect" is attributed to Richard Saul Wurman. Wurman sees architecture as "used in the words architect of foreign policy. I mean architect as in the creating of systemic, structural, and orderly principles to make something work—the thoughtful making of either artifact, or idea, or policy that informs because it is clear."

In the context of information systems design information architecture refers to the analysis and design of the data stored by information systems, concentrating on entities, their attributes, and their interrelationships. It refers to the modeling of data for an individual database and to the corporate data models an enterprise uses to coordinate the definition of data in several (perhaps scores or hundreds) of distinct databases. The "canonical data model" is applied to integration technologies as a definition for specific data passed between the systems of an enterprise. At a higher level of abstraction it may also refer to the definition of data stores.

Information architecture is defined by the R.I.P.O.S.E. technique, developed in 1989 as:

1. The conceptual structure and logical organization of the intelligence of a person or group of people (organizations). Note: In this case the term *intelligence* is used to the effect of "knowledge used to inform".

Information architecture is defined by the Information Architecture Institute as:

1. The structural design of shared information environments.
2. The art and science of organizing and labeling web sites, intranets, online communities, and software to support findability and usability.

3. An emerging community of practice focused on bringing principles of design and architecture to the digital landscape.

It is worth mentioning that the term Information Architecture has been criticized, as the term "architecture" is primarily used for habitable physical structures and imply that information systems are static like habitable physical structures or buildings. Information systems are "living systems", which frequently get updated, altered, and morphed, both by author and users. In some cases, information systems dynamically adapt to specific actions and context of users. Since the discipline of architecture ("habitable physical structures") increasingly uses materials and solutions that are less static, this criticism may be unjustified.

User-Centered Information Designers analyze cognitive, behavioral, and emotional processes of users and define User-Centered Information Systems and taxonomies. Furthermore, some activities involved in the creation of information systems can be similar to activities involved in the creation of taxonomies. Some have suggested that the term information architecture is analogous with taxonomy. Others contend that the activities involved in the creation of a taxonomy are a subset of the activities involved in developing an information architecture, since this typically also involves articulating the objectives of the information, and understanding the intended audience. Some practicing information architects specialize in developing taxonomies, as part of their IA "toolkit," along with deliverables like site maps, flow diagrams, and screen-level design prototypes to represent the structure of a Web site or interactive application.

Further, because information architecture practices and techniques became popularized with the advent of the World

Wide Web, some information architects may lack experience designing systems that are not web-based where browsing is less relevant. Users of enterprise systems and business systems typically have different goals from users of web-based systems. Business systems within the enterprise, for example, provide users with tools to expedite required business tasks. In contrast, commerce sites, social sites, and news sites invite users to explore and browse information in many cases to support their business model. It is important for Information Architects to understand the specific business and user requirements rather than apply the same techniques to shape every system's information.

Finally, with the ever increasing integration of applications within the enterprise, neither websites nor corporate data models and master data systems can any longer be considered in isolation. Information Architecture will be challenged to evolve to include the entire spectrum of both structured and unstructured data, ranging from transactional systems to ad hoc usage.

II

SERIALS CRISIS

The term serials crisis has become a common shorthand to describe the chronic subscription cost increases of many scholarly journals. The prices of these institutional or library subscriptions have been rising much faster than the Consumer Price Index for several decades, while the funds available to the libraries have remained static or have declined in real terms. As a result, academic and research libraries have regularly canceled serial subscriptions to accommodate price increases of the remaining current subscriptions.

The subscription prices of scholarly journals have been increasing at a rate faster than the inflation rate for several decades. This chronic inflation is caused by several factors. Each journal title publishes unique research findings and as a result is a unique commodity that cannot be replaced in an academic library collection by another journal title, such as less expensive journal on the same subject as one could with commodities. The publisher thus has the ability to act as a monopolist. Scholarly journals vary greatly in quality as do the individual articles that they publish. The highest quality journals are often expected and demanded by scholars to be included in their institution's library collections, often with little regard or knowledge about the subscription costs. Traditional metrics for quality in scholarly journals include Impact Factor and Citation count as recorded by Journal Citation Reports. This leads to a price inelasticity for these higher quality journals.

Another possible set of factors in this situation includes the increasing domination of scholarly communication by a small number of commercial publishers, whose journals are more costly than those of academic societies. However, it must be noted that the institutional subscription prices for journals published by many academic society publishers exihibit similar inflationary patterns as seen among commercial publishers.

An additional problem is a dramatic increase in the volume of research literature and increasing specialization of that research, academic subfields. This includes a growth in the number of scholars and increases potential demand for these journals. At the same time funds available for purchase journals are often decreasing in real terns. Libraries have seen collection budgets decline in real terms compared to the United States Periodical Price index, and there are other library expenditures such as computers and networking equipment.

Currency exchange rates can serve to increase the volatility of subscription prices throughout the world. For example, many of the publishers of scientific journals are in Europe and do not set prices in United States dollars, so the prices of such scholarly journals in the United States vary in relation to exchange rate fluctuations.

As with most issues described as a crisis, there is much discussion among those who are confronted with the crisis, in this case librarians and scholars, about the crisis and how to address its consequences. Academic and research libraries are resorting to several tactics to contain costs, while maintaining access tc the latest scholarly research for their users. These tactics include increasingly borrowing journals from one another or purchasing single articles from commercial document suppliers instead of subscribing to whole journals. Additionally, academica and research libraries cancel subscriptions to the least used or least cost-effective journals.

Another tactic has been converting from printed to electronic copies of journals, however, publishers sometimes charge more for the online edition of a journal, and price increases for online journals have followed the same inflationary pattern as have journals in paper format. Many individual libraries have joined co-operative consortia that negotiate license terms for journal subscriptions on behalf of their member institutions. Another tactic has been to encourage various methods of obtaining free access to journals.

Developed in part as a response to the serials crisis, Open access (publishing) models have included new models of financing scholarly journals that may serve to reduce the monopoly power of scholarly journal publishers which is considered a contributing factor to the creation of the serials crisis. These include: open access journals where the reader of a journal or the library at their institution does not need to pay a subscription or a pay per-view charge to read the articles published in that journal. This free access is achieved through a number of basic models. First is the publication fee model in which a funding agency, a university, or the author(s) of an article pays a publication fee per article to ensure that it will be available to readers free of charge. Sometimes these journals will waive the publication fee if the author cannot pay. Secondly, some open access journals receive institutional subsidies or are grant funded, which makes it unnecessary for the journal to charge publication or subscription fees.

This reliance on money from interested parties could conceivably lead to journals being forced to follow the agenda of the funding agency or government and thus may compromise editorial independence; however it should be noted that much of the research conducted and submitted to scholarly journals throughout the world is funded by the aforementioned interested parties. A third model is for publications to be funded by advertisements if readership of the journal is sufficient to recoup costs.

2. delayed open access journals are traditional subscription-based journals that provide open access after an embargo period from the initial publication date. A subscription or an article purchase would be required to read the materials before the end of this embargo period. These journals may additionally deposit their publications in open repositories. Many scholarly society journals have adopted this model. While this model increases access to scholarly research literature for many, academic and research libraries that continue subscriptions end up paying for access to a rolling file of the most recent material of the embargo period only.

3. hybrid open access journals are traditional subscription-based journals that permit authors to pay a fee to make their article available free of charge to the reader. This gives the author the advantages of open access to their published

research but subscribers continue to pay subscription fees for such journals to gain access to the restricted content. This model has been adopted by many of the commercial publishers and large scholarly societies. It has the potential to increase revenues for the publisher, while at the same time subjecting libraries to continuing price inflation. This model doesn't serve to end the serials crisis — unless the subscription price for a hybrid journal should decline in some fashion related to the proportion of the journal that has become open access. Oxford University Press announced on July 25th, 2007 price reductions for 2008 calendar year online-only subscriptions for its "Oxford Open Journals", however, in many cases these subscription prices are still higher than 2007 calendar year subscriptions. The price reductions are only a reduction compared with the price Oxford University Press would have charged in the absence of Open Access content. Springer Verlag has outlined its intention to develop pricing based on changes in the proportion of Open Choice (TM) articles as compared to the subscription model articles, Hypothetically, this model could serve as an intermediary step in a switch to the widescale adoption of the open access journal model.

III

Publishing has a crucial place in the librarian's ethos. To the outsider the book trade has never been easy to understand. As the structure is now being modified it is even less comprehensible and not noticeably more rational. One of the difficulties has been that traditionally the trade, or at least the publishing part of it, has been conscious of a cultural role and responsibilities, and has insisted that the publisher is not like other businessmen or manufacturers, but is concerned with other values as well as profit. This claim is not without some justification, but it has produced an ambivalence which has always affected the relationships of publishers with authors, or even librarians. Quite apart from the publishers' ideals or pretensions, it is true that there are unique features of the book trade which made analysis difficult. Books are 'different', not only because of their essential cultural role, but because a book is not a commodity in the usual economic sense, and each title is unique. One book costing £I is unlikely to be comparable in any other way as a product to another book costing the same amount. If one compares book publishing with the other communications industries, the special characteristics of the former are apparent. Unlike broadcasting or newspaper publishing, expensive plant is not required, so that small firms can enter the business. Advertising resources for each book (product) are limited by the short production runs—short in comparison to a mass circulation periodical or newspaper. Books are not necessarily mass media and quite small editions can be produced economically. The contents of books are not influenced by a dual role of advertising media, as are periodicals and newspapers.

Lastly, because of their usually compact physical form and the absence of auxiliary equipment for their use, books have several practical advantages over other media. (Their relative disadvantages, especially the loss of immediacy, are obvious, and have been touched upon in earlier chapters.) These characteristics make it possible for publishers to respond to demands for a wide variety of different material; book publishing is, therefore, a fairly flexible industry which includes many different types of activity in the act of presenting communication.

Paperback Publishing

At first sight it is very odd that a vital distinction in modern book production should be whether a book has a hard or a soft cover—particularly when one considers that in continental Europe books have traditionally been published in paper covers. The difference is that the paperback represents the impact of mass production and mass selling on an industry otherwise geared to the supply of a smaller market. It shows another aspect of the clash between *nouveau* mass culture and that of a conventional minority. It has been estimated that paperback sales in Britain now account for about sixty per cent of all book sales.

Even if we regard some paperback publishing as a medium of mass communication, a considerable part of the paperback trade now sells books which are neither cheap nor necessarily popular. Prices have increased in proportion more than they have for hardback publications, because a variety of 'quality' paperbacks are being published in relatively small editions. Publishers' own cheap reprints in the old sense have almost ceased to exist; they have been replaced by paperback editions and, in general, fewer copies of them are printed than in the paperback editions of new books. The 'egghead' paperback trade, which first developed in America and has grown in importance with the expansion of higher education, is not directed at a mass market. It takes advantages not of a mass market, but of a *known* market (students) which can be more surely attracted to buy cheap editions. Apart from the publications intended for students, particularly at the tertiary level, it should be emphasised that Penguin Books proved long ago that quality publishing in cheap paperback form can be a commercial proposition, through sales figures which in the thirties would have seemed impossible. This was the key to Penguin's success in the first instance.

The reference to Penguin, which first began publishing more than thirty years ago, serves to remind us that paperback publications are not new in Britain, but the overworked term 'paperback revolution' has been widely adopted because of the extent to which this sector of the trade has come decisively to influence the rest. In fact, many would agree with John Calder ('Some aspects of book publishing', *Library Association Record,* 1967, p. 339) that paperback publishing has 'taken over' the trade. He points out that many hardback publishers can survive only by selling paperback publishing rights in their books as quickly as possible after the contract has been signed with an author.

According to Calder, in most cases the only reason for publication in hardback form is to *obtain press reviews* which cannot be had for a paperback, and when paperbacks start to be reviewed in the same way, as presumably will happen, the trade will be 'turned upside down'. For the moment, first publication in soft covers under a paperback firm's imprint is still largely regarded as 'unserious'. There is the further significant point that most of the large British paperback companies are now American owned or controlled and they are becoming, not necessarily through 'parental' influence, very much more profit-conscious, with the resulting qualification which this imposes on the material they select to publish. There is, therefore, what might be called a crisis in publishing, and the advent of the paperback is partly responsible. Many publishers have prophesied doom for the conventional hardback trade, though from the point of view of the consumer it may seem largely irrelevant what kind of covers books have, provided that they are produced and distributed in sufficient numbers. The paperbacks does present special problems for librarians and these are discussed below.

Partly because of the paperback phenomenon, and partly for economic reasons which are not confined to the book trade, publishers have had to adopt the attitudes of 'modern' businessmen or perish. They now refer to 'marketing' and 'selling'; they are using automation in warehousing and distribution; they pay attention to exports; and, most important, they have continued to amalgamate their firms, so that eventually there may be only a few large publishing groups left in control of most of the trade. At present, six of the largest British publishing groups account for about thirty per cent of the sales. These are International Publishing Corporation, Collins, Penguin Books, Associated Book Publishers, Hutchinsons, Routledge and Kegan Paul. This trend has caused some concern. It has been suggested, notably by Raymond Williams ('Books in peril', *Library Association Record,* January 1963, p. 3), that this amalgamation process will affect the *quality* of publishing, and may make it more difficult for works of merit but no obvious commercial value to find a publisher. He stresses that the current emphasis is on *speed of sale,* and this will mean that there will be pressure *on authors* to help serve the interests of rapid selling.

It is true that book production and distribution is now being diversified, and is, to some extent, passing into the hands of people who do not value books in the way the old fashioned publishers did. Paperbacks of suitable market appeal are being distributed in supermarkets and by slot machines, as in the United States. (In this context it is of interest to note Penguin's claim that American reliance on supermarkets is not really economic, since, although there are vast sales, there is also a higher proportion of the stockholding returned unsold to the publisher—possibly as much as fifty per cent.) There has also been an increase in the use of direct selling, instead of through bookshops, as is noted below. There can be no doubt that commercialisation and amalgamation have their dangers—publishing's new technocrats are a significant portent, but whether they are a menace to civilisation remains to be seen. So far there is probably insufficient evidence to show that all Raymond Williams' fears are justified. He has on numerous occasions proposed the setting up of a 'Book Council' in order to keep publishing and bookselling in the hands of those who value books. One of its functions would be to establish (with the aid of a state capital grant) a distributive system for the selling of books. It is certainly true that many of the large companies which are moving into book publishing are not book publishers in the traditional sense at all.

Some of them, like the Thomson Organisation, are newspaper publishers. Whether a state agency—like a Book Council—is a better alternative is a matter of opinion. It should be added that although mergers take place with some frequency, there is still in existence a large number of small independent publishing units (some of the big groups allow their subsidiary imprints some measure of independence), and this is of relevance to the alleged *overproduction* in British publishing. Clive Bingley (in *Library Association Record,*) suggests that the growth is partly caused by publications being put into lists to maintain financial turnover levels while the volume of sale for individual hardback titles continues to fall. Bingley goes on to point out that the long term trend of hardcover sales to individuals is downwards, and argues that there is a causal relationship between this fact and the rising levels of book prices. He analyses the other reasons for price increases in some detail, as does a statement by the Publishers Association in the same issue of the LAR, p. 75. This statement admits that price increases are continual, but concludes 'What is maintained is that across the board these increases are not unreasonable and that British books are not highly priced and remain the cheaper unsubsidised books in the world outside the Soviet bloc.'

Many public librarians, bothered by local government committees, fail to appreciate either the justice of the increases or the reasons for them. It may be that publishers should have increased their prices dramatically long ago in preference to the recent steady creep, which has been estimated to be at the rate of roughly ten per cent a year during the 1960's. The trade has long been afflicted by social attitudes to books which cause people to expect them to remain cheap even when other commodities continue to rise in price. It is possible, and a point of much debate, that the knowledge that books can be borrowed free, whereas other items cannot, causes even the reading public to feel that the purchase of a new book is a greater extravagance than buying a bottle of whisky for the same amount of money.

Growth of Exports

It is to be noted that one postwar development has seen books become an important export industry. The Publishers Association, encouraged by the government, responded to the trade's awareness of the importance to its future of expanding export markets, by setting up in 1966 the *Book Development Council* to promote book exports abroad. It appears that none of the available trade statistics can be accepted without qualification, but it may be safe to say that at least half the books sold annually by British publishers go abroad. Overseas markets have become vital, and Macmillan's for example, have made an interesting and controversial innovation by co-operating with several African governments in establishing and developing their state publishing enterprises.

The Bookshop Crisis

Remarkably, the outstanding trend in modern bookselling has been a decline in the number of good bookshops of the traditional kind—reflecting perhaps the decline in hardcover book sales already mentioned. Many towns do not now have a good bookshop at all, and even in London many of the best shops have closed down. It has been estimated that eighty per cent of the UK bookselling trade goes to ten per cent of the booksellers, and that the remaining twenty per cent (mostly single copies) goes to the rest. Of all books bought it is probable that only about one half are sold over the counter in bookshops. Chain stores like W.H. Smith and Son Ltd. do not offer a service comparable with that of the traditional bookshop. In the United States, bookshops of the old type are not often found, but numerous alternative outlets exist, and, as Calder notes (in the article already quoted), you can buy a book in about every fifth building in a large town. In Britain, however, the booksellers are declining in number, and the new outlets which might replace them do not yet exist in sufficient quantity; in addition, many people in the trade do not want these new outlets.

They are not, after all, part of the traditional book trade at all. Even so, diversification is likely to increase and, as far as booksellers proper are concerned, there is likely to be a move towards the consolidation of existing shops into larger groups to face the competition, and a greater reliance on mail order selling. Those who appreciate the cultural value of a good bookshop in the life of a community must regret their gradual disappearance. A reason for the decline of small bookshops, and a sound justification of consolidation among them, is that the large number of books now in print has meant that many of the small bookshops are incapable of holding a broad enough range of stock to retain general custom; this is one of the acknowledged functions of the bookshop (the other being the provision of bibliographical information, so that books can be ordered). It may be that it is the marketing difference between the bookshop and the new mass retail outlets that is now a more important factor in the organisation of the trade than the disintegrating distinction (for business purposes) between hardcover and paperback books. (For example, publications first issued in paperback are now often reissued in hard cover editions, instead of vice-versa; also, many publishers, especially the university presses, issue books simultaneously in soft and hardcover editions.)

Publishers and booksellers now depend on libraries' custom, particularly public libraries, far more than even before. There has been enormous increase in hardcover *reading* in recent years, even though book buying by private individuals has declined. The majority of this reading is through the agency of public libraries, which lend approximately 500 million books a year. One quarter of all books which are bought in the UK is bought by public libraries, representing a spending power of £15 million annually. Because of the increasing importance of the library market, the book trade has increased its contacts with libraries in a number of areas. There has been fruitful co-operation, and inevitably some friction, on particular issues. The following are some of the most noticeable developments.

Decline of Subscription Libraries

Ever since the eighteenth century, subscription libraries have played a significant role in British social life, and throughout the nineteenth century they provided literature for middle class people who did not use the public libraries. With the arrival of the railway age, Charles Edward Mudie established in 1842 what was to become a nation-wide network of subscription libraries, and later the firm of W.H. Smith followed suit. The early twentieth century saw the establishment of Boots' 'Booklovers Library', the Time Book Club in London, and libraries in a number of department stores such as Harrods. In addition to these commercial circulating libraries, there were in most of the large provincial towns what can best be called 'proprietary subscription libraries', which maintained a permanent stock: these also date from the eighteenth century. The London Library was founded in 1841—a library which for intellectual workers, particularly writers, has provided a service which cannot be equalled by public libraries. It is perhaps for this reason that, in spite of continuing financial difficulties, the London Library alone remains the best known of these ventures.

There were undoubtedly economic factors as well. As far as public libraries are concerned, readers who formerly used subscription libraries have increased the demand for certain types of 'middlebrow' literature, and placed a heavier burden on reservation or request systems. These are the kinds of people who arrive in the library on Monday mornings with a list of requests compiled from the review columns of the Sunday papers. This demand has been called 'best-seller pressure', and by some librarians condemned—a curious professional example of the puritanic attitude. The point is worth stressing, because students of librarianship commonly suppose that the subscription libraries simply dispensed light literature, and presume that their demise has transferred the light fiction 'problem' to the public libraries; if this is really a problem, it is one which has always been there. It is true, but only partly relevant, that subscription libraries did provide light novels, and there are still small stationers who run a 'library' service wholly devoted to this kind of literature. What is relevant, perhaps, is that public librarians can no longer employ the argument that those who require light fiction should go to the subscription libraries. Otherwise, the main impact of this situation has been the need to increase the number of copies purchased of books which are currently news.

Book Clubs

In the United States, book clubs offering cut price editions of selected titles to a subscribing membership represent a large trade outlet. Because of quasi-legal agreements concerning the sale of new books in club editions, book clubs in the UK have hitherto been of lesser importance. In 1968, however, the discovery of a technical loophole, and subsequent hasty ratification of it by the trade, made it possible to publish new books simultaneously in trade and book club editions. An increase in this type of publishing seems likely.

Joint Working Party

After a conference initiated by the North-Western Polytechnic School of Librarianship in 1965, a Working Party for Library and Book Trade Relations was set up, with Peter Wright, then lecturer at the school, as chairman. The working party was concerned about the fact that, although librarians and members of the book trade have common aims, their attitudes and their methods are frequently in conflict. This was an *ad hoc* informal body which was interested in practical results, and its most important achievement so far has been the introduction in 1968 of PICS, the Publishers' Information Card Service.

This project is a commercial undertaking, with editorial services supplied by Whitaker's, the bibliographical publishing firm. Essentially the scheme provides a centralised information service about new books, with the information presented on standard cards designed eventually to replace much of the diverse publicity material which individual publishers circulate. The service is free to receiving libraries, and the publishers pay £10 for each title for which they wish to have a card printed. The cards are, as far as possible, advance notices of publication compiled from information supplied by the publishers. The information given includes not only the title but scope, contents, readership, a note on the author and the standard book number. The administrative and practical advantages of this service, both for librarians and publishers, are readily apparent; booksellers could also find uses for the cards. As G.R. Davies points out (*Library Association Record*, January 1969, p. 8), the book trade had not sufficiently realised that, although forceful publicity may be an appropriate means of promoting sales to private individuals, it is not helpful to librarians. In addition, publicity material is issued at random times in all shapes and sizes, from hundreds of publishers, and it cannot rely on individual attention from librarians. It represents in many cases the production of expensive material destined straight for the wastepaper basket. Davies also notes that the production of PIC cards by publishers themselves is not a practical proposition; a centralised system is required, and in fact costs each participating publisher less than if it were to be done by himself.

IV

PUBLIC LENDING RIGHT

The long standing discussion on the establishment of a public lending right for authors represents one area where the book trade and librarians have not agreed. Just as a composer or a dramatist receives payment under performing rights legislation whenever his work is performed in public, so authors have sought to establish their right to an analogous public lending right, by which they would receive a payment when books are borrowed by public library readers. There have been a variety of different proposals since 1951, when John Brophy first suggested that for every loan of a public library book its author should receive one penny. These have included the similar proposals incorporated in a Society of Authors' pamphlet *Critical times for authors* (1953), and a memorandum drawn up by A.P. Herbert under the auspices of a special committee of the Authors' and Publishers' Lending Rights Association. This memorandum, published in 1960, surveyed the practical difficulties of setting up a workable scheme, and noted the objections of librarians. It recommended that a

Bill should be presented to parliament, to amend the Copyright Act of 1956 for the establishment of PLR under the aegis of the (then) Ministry of Education. In 1960, Woodrow Wyatt presented the first PLR Bill to the House of Commons. This was based on the penny per-issue principle, but the government would not support the proposals, and it was decided to abandon any attempt to relate PLR to copyright legislation. A second Bill was drafted, and presented by William Teeling, but the opposition remained too strong and it was duly 'talked out'—in November 1960, and again in March 1961. Meanwhile, the Library Association had expressed total opposition to the scheme, which this time proposed that the library authorities should be allowed an option to charge borrowers. Following this second failure, the campaign continued, and included a motion in the House of Commons (1961) and a booklet by A.P. Herbert called *Libraries: free for all?* This last suggested that public libraries should make a maximum annual charge to registered readers of *7s 6d* per head. There was also an attempt, which failed, to introduced an amendment to the Public Libraries Bill of 1964.

Further impetus was given to the campaign by the publication in 1965 of the government white paper, 'A policy for the arts', produced by Miss Jennie Lee, minister with the responsibility for the arts. She subsequently showed herself sympathetic to the idea of PLR, but rejected any proposals which invalidated the concept of the 'free' public library. In principle she found Scandinavian practice more acceptable, since these schemes do not involve payment by public-library users.

The next stage was the setting up in 1965 of a working party by the Arts Council of Great Britain, to consider all aspects of PLR. The initiative thus finally passed out of the hands of the Authors' and Publishers' Lending Right

Association (APLA), which had sustained the campaign for six years. During the period it had become evident that proposals which involved payment by the public or by the local authorities could not gain acceptance. This working party sent their report to the Department of Education and Science in 1967, and the scheme which it proposes involves a grant from central government funds, on the basis of fifteen per cent of the annual sum spent on books by library authorities. The amount available would then be divided, with seventy five per cent going to authors and twenty five per cent to publishers (previous proposals have not always included the publishers). The use by libraries would be calculated, not on any figures for the number of times a book is borrowed, but on *stock held*. To obtain the required information, three representative library authorities would each year be sent a list of all books in copyright, and they would send in a return showing how many of these books were in stock. In the words of a Society of Authors leaflet, the PLR committee to be set up by the Department of Education and Science to run the scheme would then 'gross up these sample returns in the ratio they bore to the total stock of all library authorities in the country'. The leaflet claims that Danish experience suggests that this might yield approximately 10*d* a book, 'so that, on 2,000 copies of a single title held by public libraries throughout the country, an author would receive £85 a year'. It will be apparent that the scheme is strongly based on the Danish principle.

During 1969, several statements were made by government spokesmen indicating that there was official sympathy for the Arts Council schemes, but that, in the words of Baroness Phillips, 'the government tend to have an open mind but a closed purse'. Later, in reply to a parliamentary question, Miss Jennie Lee, the minister responsible, said that there were alternative proposals to be considered, and that a working party would be set up. It therefore appears that there will be yet another working party report before a solution is found, but the present evidence suggests that eventually some form of PLR will emerge. There is not need to summarise here the arguments for and against PLR, for during the controversy they have been constantly repeated. Certain comments, however, are called for. What must strike any impartial observer is that this campaign has taken eighteen years to come anywhere near the possibility of a successful conclusion, and one reason for this has been the total lack of co-operation between the Library Association on one hand, and the bodies representing the authors on the other. (Publishers have been sympathetic to the idea, and have, naturally, pressed their own claims.) Many of the earliest proposals, which were impractical both from an administrative and political point of view, might not have been pursued for so long if librarians had shown themselves at once to be more sympathetic or co-operative to the principle. At no time has the organised profession admitted that the authors have any kind of a case, and some of the statements by individual librarians published in the press have betrayed an almost paranoiac antipathy towards writers, for reasons which it would be uncharitable to pursue. The Library Association did at one time meet representatives of APLA (1962), but this has been the limit of professional concern. (The LA stated that it could not accept representation on the 1965 PLR working party because the local authority associations were not represented. In January 1968 the Association of Municipal Corporations announced their unqualified opposition to any PLR scheme, particularly if publishers were to be, in their words, 'subsidised'.)

The Net Book Agreement

The Net Book Agreement, which allows publishers to establish and maintain the prices at which their new books may be sold, has survived a fair amount of hostile criticism, as well as an investigation in 1962 by the Restrictive Practices Court, which gave judgment in its favour. Public libraries therefore continue to purchase books at the ten per cent discount provided for under the library Licence Agreement, which was revised by the Publishers Association in 1964. The Court concluded that, in general, public libraries would not benefit from the abrogation of the Net Book Agreement. Nevertheless, in view of the continued rise in book prices, many librarians have claimed hat the ten per cent discount off publishers' prices is insufficient. Some publishers also criticise the Net Book Agreement on the ground that it serves to subsidise inefficient booksellers.

REFERENCES

1. Dingley, Brenda. US. Periodical Prices – 2005.
2. Judith M. Panitch and Sarah Michalak. The Serials Crisis: A White Paper for the UNC-Chapel Hill Scholarly Communications Convocation, January, 2005.

9

Intellectual Property and Copyright

"The man who graduates today and stops learning tomorow is uneducated the day after."

—Newten D. Baker

"Stable ownership is the gift of social law, and is given late in the progress of society. It would be curious then, if an idea, the fugitive fermentation of an individual brain, could, of natural right, be claimed in exclusive and stable property. If nature has made any one thing less susceptible than all others of exclusive property, it is the action of the thinking power called an idea, which an individual may exclusively possess as long as he keeps it to himself; but the moment it is divulged, it forces itself into the possession of every one, and the receiver cannot dispossess himself of it. Its peculiar character, too, is that no one possesses the less, because every other possesses the whole of it. He who receives an idea from me, receives instruction himself without lessening mine; as he who lights his taper at mine, receives light without darkening me. That ideas should freely spread from one to another over the globe, for the moral and mutual instruction of man, and improvement of his condition, seems to have been peculiarly and benevolently designed by nature, when she made them, like fire, expansible over all space, without lessening their density in any point, and like the air in which we breathe, move,

> and have our physical being, incapable of confinement or exclusive appropriation. Inventions then cannot, in nature, be a subject of property."
>
> —*Thomas Jefferson, to Isaac McPherson*
> *13 Aug. 1813 Writings 13:333—35*

In fact, modern usage of the term intellectual property goes back at least as far as 1888 with the founding in Berne of the Swiss Federal Office for Intellectual Property (the Bureau fédéral de la propriété intellectuelle). When the administrative secretariats established by the Paris Convention (1883) and the Berne Convention (1886) merged in 1893, they also located in Berne, and also adopted the term intellectual property in their new combined title, the United International Bureaux for the Protection of Intellectual Property. The organisation subsequently relocated to Geneva in 1960, and was succeeded in 1967 with the establishment of the World Intellectual Property Organization (WIPO) by treaty as an agency of the United Nations. According to Lemley, it was only at this point that the term really began to be used in the United States (which had not been a party to the Berne Convention), and it did not enter popular usage until passage of the Bayh-Dole Act in 1980. The concept appears to have made its first appearance after the French revolution. In an 1818 collection of his writings, the French liberal theorist, Benjamin Constant, argued against the recently-introduced idea of "property which has been called intellectual." The term intellectual property can be found used in an October 1845 Massachusetts Circuit Court ruling in the patent case Davoll et al. v. Brown., in which Justice Charles L. Woodbury wrote that "only in this way can we protect intellectual property, the labors of the mind, productions and interests are as much a man's own...as the wheat he cultivates, or the flocks he rears." The statement that "discoveries are...property" goes back earlier. Section 1 of the French law of 1791 stated, "All new discoveries are the property of the author; to assure the inventor the property and temporary enjoyment of his discovery, there shall be delivered to him a patent for five, ten or fifteen years." The concept's origins can potentially be traced back further. Jewish law includes several considerations whose effects are similar to those of modern intellectual property laws, though the notion of intellectual creations as property does not seem to exist – notably the principle of Hasagat Ge'vul (unfair encroachment) was used to justify limited-term publisher (but not author) copyright in the 16th century. The Talmud contains the prohibitions against certain mental crimes (further elaborated in the Shulchan Aruch), notably Geneivat da'at (literally "mind theft"), which some have interpreted as prohibiting theft of ideas, though the doctrine is principally concerned with fraud and deception, not property.

Intellectual property (IP) is a number of distinct types of legal monopolies over creations of the mind, both artistic and commercial, and the corresponding fields of law. Under intellectual property law, owners are granted certain exclusive rights to a variety of intangible assets, such as musical, literary, and artistic works; ideas, discoveries and inventions; and words, phrases, symbols, and designs. Common types of intellectual property include copyrights, trademarks, patents, industrial design rights and trade secrets in some jurisdictions. Although many of the legal principles governing intellectual property have evolved over centuries, it was not until the 19th century that the term *intellectual property* began to be used, and, it is said, not until the late 20th century that it became commonplace in the United States.

Intellectual property rights are a bundle of exclusive rights over creations of the mind, both artistic and commercial. The former is covered by copyright laws, which protect creative works, such as books, movies, music, paintings, photographs, and software, and give the copyright holder exclusive right to control reproduction or adaptation of such works for a certain period of time.

The second category is collectively known as "industrial properties", as they are typically created and used for industrial or commercial purposes. A patent may be granted for a new, useful, and non-obvious invention and gives the patent holder a right to prevent others from practicing the invention without a license from the inventor for a certain period of time. A trademark is a distinctive sign which is used to prevent confusion among products in the marketplace.

An industrial design right protects the form of appearance, style or design of an industrial object from infringement. A trade secret is an item of non-public information concerning the commercial practices or proprietary knowledge of a business. Public disclosure of trade secrets may sometimes be illegal. The term intellectual property denotes the specific legal rights described above, and not the intellectual work itself.

In fact, these exclusive rights allow owners of intellectual property to reap monopoly profits. These monopoly profits provide a financial incentive for the creation of intellectual property, and pay associated research and development costs. Some commentators, such as David Levine and Michele Boldrin, dispute this justification.

The legal monopoly granted by IP laws are credited with significant contributions toward economic growth. Economists estimate that two-thirds of the value of large businesses in the U.S. can be traced to intangible assets. Industries which rely on IP protections are estimated to produce 72 percent more value added per employee than non-IP industries. A joint research project of the WIPO and the United Nations University measuring the impact of IP systems on six Asian countries found "a positive correlation between the strengthening of the IP system and subsequent economic growth." However, correlation does not necessarily mean causation: given that the patent holders can freely relocate, the Nash equilibrium predicts they will obviously prefer operating in countries with strong IP laws. In some of the cases, the economic growth that comes with a stronger IP system is due to increase in stock capital from direct foreign investment, as was shown for Taiwan after the 1986 reform.

Further, it is worthmentioning that the Intellectual property rights are temporary monopolies enforced by the state regarding use of expressions and ideas. Intellectual property rights are usually limited to non-rival goods, that is, goods which can be used or enjoyed by many people simultaneously—the use by one person does not exclude use by another. This is compared to rival goods, such as clothing, which may only be used by one person at a time.

For example, any number of people may make use of a mathematical formula simultaneously. Some objections to the term intellectual property are based on the argument that property can only properly be applied to rival goods (or that one cannot "own" property of this sort). Since a non-rival good may be used (copied, for example) by many simultaneously (produced with minimal marginal cost), producers would need incentives other than money to create such works. Monopolies, by contrast, also have inefficiencies (producers will charge more and produce less than would be socially desirable). The establishment of intellectual property rights, therefore, represents a trade-off, to balance the interest of society in the creation of non-rival goods (by encouraging their production) with the problems of monopoly power.

Since the trade-off and the relevant benefits and costs to society will depend on many factors that may be specific to each product and society, the optimum period of time during which the temporary monopoly rights should exist is unclear.

A Critical Analysis

Although the term is in wide use, some critics reject the term *intellectual property* altogether. Richard Stallman argues that it "systematically distorts and confuses these issues, and its use was and is promoted by those who gain from this confusion." He claims that the term "operates as a catch-all to lump together disparate laws [which] originated separately, evolved differently, cover different activities, have different rules, and raise different public policy issues."

These critics advocate referring to copyrights, patents and trademarks in the singular and warn against abstracting disparate laws into a collective term. Some critics of intellectual property, such as those in the free culture movement, point at intellectual monopolies as harming health, preventing progress, and benefiting concentrated interests to the detriment of the masses, and argue that the public interest is harmed by ever expansive monopolies in the form of copyright extensions, software patents and business method patents.

Other criticism of intellectual property law concerns the tendency of the protections of intellectual property to expand, both in duration and in scope. The trend has been toward longer copyright protection (raising fears that it may some day be eternal). In addition, the developers and controllers of items of intellectual property have sought to bring more items under the protection. Patents have been granted for living organisms, and colors have been trademarked. Because they are systems of government-granted monopolies copyrights, patents, and trademarks are called intellectual monopoly privileges, (IMP) a topic on which several academics, including Birgitte Andersen and Thomas Alured Faunce have written.

Now we will come to copyright and legal measures for its protection.

COPYRIGHT

In common parlance, Copyright is a form of intellectual property that gives the author of an original work exclusive right for a certain time period in relation to that work, including its publication, distribution and adaptation, after which time the work is said to enter the public domain. Copyright applies to any expressible form of an idea or information that is substantive and discrete and fixed in a medium. Some jurisdictions also recognize "moral rights" of the creator of a work, such as the right to be credited for the work. Copyright is described under the umbrella term intellectual property along with patents and trademarks. An example of the intent of copyright, as expressed in the United States Constitution, is "To promote the Progress of Science and useful Arts, by securing for limited Times to Authors and Inventors the exclusive Right to their respective Writings and Discoveries."

It is pertinent to note that Copyright has been internationally standardized, lasting between fifty to a hundred years from the author's death, or a shorter period for anonymous or corporate authorship. Some jurisdictions have required formalities to establish copyright, but most recognize copyright in any completed work, without formal registration. Generally, copyright is enforced as a civil matter, though some jurisdictions do apply criminal sanctions.

Basically, the concept of copyright originates with the Statute of Anne (1710) in Britain. It established the author of a work as the owner of the right to copy that work and the concept of a fixed term for that copyright. It was created as an act "for the encouragement of learning", as it had been noted at the time that publishers were reprinting the works of authors without their consent "to their very great detriment, and too often to the Ruin of them and their Families". As such, copyright was first created with the intention that authors might have some control over the printing of their work and to receive some financial recompense, so that this would encourage them to write more books and thus to aid the flow of ideas and learning. As the act itself says: "for the encouragement of learned men to compose and write useful books". The Statute of Anne was the first real copyright act, and gave the authors rights for a fixed period, a fourteen year term for all works published under the statute, after which the copyright expired. Copyright has grown from a legal concept regulating copying rights in the publishing of books and maps to one with a significant effect on nearly every modern industry, covering such items as sound recordings, films, photographs, software, and architectural works. Subsequently the Copyright Clause of the United States Constitution (1787) authorized copyright legislation: "To promote the Progress of Science..., by securing for limited Times to Authors.... the exclusive Right to their... Writings."

Berne Convention for the Protection of Literary and Artistic Works

The 1886 Berne Convention first established recognition of copyrights among sovereign nations, rather than merely bilaterally. Under the Berne Convention, copyrights for creative works do not have to be asserted or declared, as they are automatically in force at creation. In these countries, there is no requirement for an author to "register" or "apply for" a copyright, or to mark his or her works with a copyright symbol or other legend. As soon as a work is "fixed", that is, written or recorded on some physical medium, its author is automatically entitled to all copyrights in the work, and to any derivative works unless and until the author explicitly disclaims them, or until the copyright expires. The Berne Convention also resulted in foreign authors being treated equivalently to domestic authors, in any country signed onto the Convention. The UK signed the Berne Convention in 1887 but did not implement large parts of it until a century later with the passage of the *Copyright, Designs and Patents Act of 1988*. The USA did not sign the Berne Convention until 1989.

Further, the United States and most Latin American countries instead entered into the Buenos Aires Convention in 1910, which required a copyright notice (such as "all rights reserved") on the work, and permitted signatory nations to limit the duration of copyrights to shorter and renewable terms. The Universal Copyright Convention was drafted in 1952 as another less demanding alternative to the Berne Convention, and ratified by nations such as the Soviet Union and developing nations.

Anti-Counterfeiting Trade Agreement

The Anti-Counterfeiting Trade Agreement (ACTA) is a proposed plurilateral trade agreement which is claimed by its proponents to be in response "to the increase in global trade of counterfeit goods and pirated copyright protected works."[4] The scope of ACTA is broad, including counterfeit physical goods, as well as "internet distribution and information technology". In October 2007 the United States, the European Community, Switzerland and Japan announced that they would negotiate ACTA. Furthermore the following countries have joined the negotiations: Australia, the Republic of Korea, New Zealand, Mexico, Jordan, Morocco, Singapore, the United Arab Emirates and Canada. The ACTA negotiations have been largely conducted in secrecy, with very little information being officially disclosed. However, on 22 May 2008 a discussion paper about the proposed agreement was uploaded to Wikileaks, and newspaper reports about the secret negotiations quickly followed.

Copyright laws have been standardized to some extent through international conventions such as the Berne Convention and Universal Copyright Convention. These multilateral treaties have been ratified by nearly all countries, and international organizations such as the European Union or World Trade Organization require their member states to comply with them. Although there are consistencies among nations' intellectual property laws, each jurisdiction has separate and distinct laws and regulations about copyright. The World Intellectual Property Organization summarizes each of its member states' intellectual property laws on its website.

Remarkable, to regulations of the Berne Convention are incorporated into the World Trade Organization's TRIPS agreement (1995), thus giving the Berne Convention effectively near-global application. The 2002 WIPO Copyright Treaty enacted greater restrictions on the use of technology to copy works in the nations that ratified it.

The British Statute of Anne, full title "An Act for the Encouragement of Learning, by Vesting the Copies of Printed Books in the Authors or Purchasers of such Copies, during the Times therein mentioned", was the first act to directly protect the rights of authors. Since its inception, copyright is considered a property right and attempts to balance the rights of the producer with the rights of society at large.

According to the World Intellectual Property Organisation (WIPO), intellectual property laws, which includes industrial property and copyright, exist for primarily two reasons:

> "One is to give statutory expression to the moral and economic rights of creators in their creations and to the rights of the public in accessing those creations. The second is to promote creativity, and the dissemination and application of its results, and to encourage fair trade, which would contribute to economic and social development."

Under US copyright law, the justification appears in the constitutional provision authorizing Congress to enact copyright laws: Article I, section 8, clause 8 provides that "Congress shall have Power ... To promote the Progress of Science ... by securing for limited Times to Authors ... the exclusive Right to their ... Writings." The term "science" has been interpreted to refer to human knowledge in general. The justification for US copyright is thus seen to be that the prospect of copyright grants encourages authors to make public their writings, which will then become a part of the public domain after a limited period. The theory that copyright is a natural property right of authors has been rejected in a series of decisions of the U.S. Supreme Court beginning with Wheaton v. Peters (1834).

Application

Copyright may apply to a wide range of creative, intellectual, scientific, or artistic forms, or "works". Specifics vary by jurisdiction, but these can include poems, theses, plays, other literary works, movies, dances, musical compositions, audio recordings, paintings, drawings, sculptures, photographs, software, radio and television and broadcasts. Copyright does not cover ideas and information themselves, only the form or manner in which they are expressed. For example, the copyright to a Mickey Mouse cartoon restricts others from making copies of the cartoon or creating derivative works based on Disney's particular anthropomorphic mouse, but it does not prohibit the creation of other works about anthropomorphic mice in general, so long as they're not copies or adaptations of Disney's mouse. In many jurisdictions, copyright law makes exceptions to these restrictions when the work is copied for the purpose of commentary or other related uses. However, other laws — such as trademark and patent law — may impose additional restrictions that copyright does not.

Typically, a work must meet minimal standards of originality in order to qualify for copyright, and the copyright expires after a set period of time (some jurisdictions may allow this to be extended). Different countries impose different tests, although generally the requirements are low; in the United Kingdom there has to be some 'skill, labour and judgment' that has gone into it.

In Australia and the United Kingdom it has been held that a single word is insufficient to comprise a copyright work. However, single words or a short string of words can sometimes be registered as a trademark instead. Copyright law recognizes the right of an author based on whether the work actually is an original creation, rather than based on whether it is unique; two authors may own copyright on two substantially identical works, if it is determined that the duplication was coincidental, and neither was copied from the other. In all countries where the Berne Convention standards apply, copyright is automatic, and need not be obtained through official registration with any government office. Once an idea has been reduced to tangible form, for example by securing it in a fixed medium (such as a drawing, sheet music, photograph, a videotape, or a computer file), the copyright holder is entitled to enforce his or her exclusive rights. However, while registration isn't needed to exercise copyright, in jurisdictions where the laws provide for registration, it serves as prima facie evidence of a valid copyright and enables the copyright holder to seek statutory damages and attorney's fees. The original holder of the copyright may be the employer of the author rather than the author himself, if the work is a "work for hire".

For example, in English law the Copyright, Designs and Patents Act 1988 provides that if a copyrighted work is made by an employee in the course of that employment, the copyright is automatically owned by the employer as a "Work for Hire." Copyrights are generally enforced by the holder in a civil law court, but there are also criminal infringement statutes in some jurisdictions. While central registries are kept in some countries, which aid in proving claims of ownership, registering does not necessarily prove ownership, nor does the fact of copying (even without permission) necessarily prove that copyright was infringed. Criminal sanctions are generally aimed at serious counterfeiting activity, but are now becoming more commonplace as copyright collectives such as the RIAA are increasingly targeting the file sharing home Internet user. Thus far, however, most such cases against file sharers have been settled out of court.

It is remarkable here that because of the cost associated with copyright registration some creators, particularly musicians, have attempted to establish evidence of ownership and creation of a work by mailing it to themselves. In the US this non-statutory practice became known as "poor man's copyright." Today the US Copyright Office makes it clear that the technique is no substitute for actual copyright registration, although the practice may be accepted as proof of creation in a number of national jurisdictions, such as the UK and the Netherlands. "Poor man's copyright" may also include depositing a copy of the work with a bank or attorney.

Exclusive Rights

The Following are some of the several exclusive rights typically attach to the holder of a copyright:

(a) to produce copies or reproductions of the work and to sell those copies (mechanical rights; including, sometimes, electronic copies: distribution rights)

(b) to transmit or display by radio or video (broadcasting rights)

(c) to import or export the work

(d) to create derivative works (works that adapt the original work)

(e) to perform or display the work publicly (performance rights)

(f) to sell or assign these rights to others

Here the phrase "exclusive right," means that only the copyright holder has a legal power to secure relief from a court against certain, statutorily defined uses by others without the copyright holder's authorization. The copyright holder is free to exercise those rights, unless doing so would violate rights of others. Copyright is sometimes called a "negative right" or "exclusionary right," as it serves to *prohibit* or *exclude* other people (e.g., readers, viewers, or listeners, and primarily publishers and would-be publishers) from doing something they would otherwise be able to do, rather than *permitting* people (e.g., authors) to do something they would otherwise be unable to do. In this way it is similar to the unregistered design right in English law and European law.

The rights of the copyright holder also permit him/her to *not* use or exploit their copyright, for some or all of the term. There is, however, a critique that rejects this assertion as being based on a philosophical interpretation of copyright law that is not universally shared. There is also debate on whether copyright should be considered a property right or a moral right. Many argue that copyright does not exist merely to restrict third parties from publishing ideas and information, and that defining copyright purely as a negative right is incompatible with the public policy objective of encouraging authors to create new works and enrich the public domain. The right to adapt a work means to transform the way in which the work is expressed. Examples include developing a stage play or film script from a novel, translating a short story, and making a new arrangement of a musical work.

Longevity

Copyright subsists for a variety of lengths in different jurisdictions. The length of the term can depend on several factors, including the type of work (e.g. musical composition, novel), whether the work has been published or not, and whether the work was created by an individual or a corporation. In most of the world, the default length of copyright is the life of the author plus either 50 or 70 years. In the United States, the term for most existing works is a fixed number of years after the date of creation or publication. In some countries (for example, the United States and the United Kingdom), copyrights expire at the end of the calendar year in question. The length and requirements for copyright duration are subject to change by legislation, and since the early 20th century there have been a number of adjustments made in various countries, which can make determining the duration of a given copyright somewhat difficult.

For example, the United States used to require copyrights to be renewed after 28 years to stay in force, and formerly required a copyright notice upon first publication to gain coverage. In Italy and France, there were post-wartime extensions that could increase the term by approximately 6 years in Italy and up to about 14 in France. Many countries have extended the length of their copyright terms (sometimes retroactively). International treaties establish minimum terms for copyrights, but individual countries may enforce longer terms than those.

Immanuel Kant in his 1785 essay *Von der Unrechtmäßigkeit des Büchernachdrucks* distinguishes the physical from the ideological, the thought involved from the book. This distinction is of critical importance to the near constant wrangling between publishers, other intermediaries, and the original, creative authors.

Copyright law does *not* restrict the owner of a copy from reselling legitimately obtained copies of copyrighted works, provided that those copies were originally produced by or with the permission of the copyright holder. It is therefore legal, for example, to resell a copyrighted book or CD. In the United States this is known as the first-sale doctrine, and was established by the courts to clarify the legality of reselling books in second-hand bookstores. Some countries may have parallel importation restrictions that allow the copyright holder to control the aftermarket. This may mean for example that a copy of a book that does not infringe copyright in the country where it was printed does infringe copyright in a country into which it is imported for retailing.

The first-sale doctrine is known as exhaustion of rights in other countries and is a principle that also applies, though somewhat differently, to patent and trademark rights. It is important to note that the first-sale doctrine permits the transfer of the particular legitimate copy involved. It does not permit making or distributing additional copies. In addition, copyright, in most cases, does not prohibit one from acts such as modifying, defacing, or destroying his or her own legitimately obtained copy of a copyrighted work, so long as duplication is not involved. However, in countries that implement moral rights, a copyright holder can in some cases successfully prevent the mutilation or destruction of a work that is publicly visible.

Fair Use and Fair Dealing

It must be remembered that copyright does not prohibit all copying or replication. In the United States, the fair use doctrine, codified by the Copyright Act of 1976 as 17 U.S.C. § 107, permits some copying and distribution without permission of the copyright holder or payment to same. The statute does not clearly define fair use, but instead gives four non-exclusive factors to consider in a fair use analysis.

Those factors are:

1. the purpose and character of the use;
2. the nature of the copyrighted work;
3. the amount and substantiality of the portion used in relation to the copyrighted work as a whole; and
4. the effect of the use upon the potential market for or value of the copyrighted work.

In the United Kingdom and many other Commonwealth countries, a similar notion of fair dealing was established by the courts or through legislation. The concept is sometimes not well defined; however in Canada, private copying for personal use has been expressly permitted by statute since 1999. In Australia, the fair dealing exceptions under the *Copyright Act 1968* (Cth) are a limited set of circumstances under which copyrighted material can be legally copied or adapted without the copyright holder's consent. Fair dealing uses are research and study; review and critique; news reportage and the giving of professional advice (i.e. legal advice).

Under current Australian law it is still a breach of copyright to copy, reproduce or adapt copyright material for personal or private use without permission from the copyright owner. Other technical exemptions from infringement may also apply, such as the temporary reproduction of a work in machine readable form for a computer. In the United States the AHRA (Audio Home Recording Act Codified in Section 10, 1992) prohibits action against consumers making noncommercial recordings of music, in return for royalties on both media and devices plus mandatory copy-control mechanisms on recorders.

Section 1008. Prohibition on certain infringement actions

> *No action ever may be brought under this title alleging infringement of copyright based on the manufacture, importation, or distribution of a digital audio recording device, a digital audio recording medium, an analog recording device, or an analog recording medium, or based on the noncommercial use by a consumer of such a device or medium for making digital musical recordings or analog musical recordings.*

Later acts amended US Copyright law so that for certain purposes making 10 copies or more is construed to be commercial, but there is no general rule permitting such copying. Indeed making one complete copy of a work, or in many cases using a portion of it, for commercial purposes will not be considered fair use.

The Digital Millennium Copyright Act prohibits the manufacture, importation, or distribution of devices whose intended use, or only significant commercial use, is to bypass an access or copy control put in place by a copyright owner.

An appellate court has held that fair use is not a defense to engaging in such distribution. Educational use is regarded as "fair use" in most jurisdictions, but the restrictions vary wildly from nation to nation.

Recent Israeli District Court decision dated Sep. 2, 2009 accepted the defence of fair use for a site linking to P2P live feeds of soccer matches. The main resoning was based on the public importance of certain sporting events, i.e. - the public's rights as counter weight to the copyright holders rights.

It worth mentioning that copyright, or aspects of it, may be assigned or transferred from one party to another. For example, a musician who records an album will often sign an agreement with a record company in which the musician agrees to transfer all copyright in the recordings in exchange for royalties and other considerations. The creator (and original copyright holder) benefits, or expects to, from production and marketing capabilities far beyond those of the author. In the digital age of music, music may be copied and distributed at minimal cost through the Internet, however the record industry attempts to provide promotion and marketing for the artist and his or her work so it can reach a much larger audience.

A copyright holder need not transfer all rights completely, though many publishers will insist. Some of the rights may be transferred, or else the copyright holder may grant another party a non-exclusive license to copy and/or distribute the work in a particular region or for a specified period of time. A transfer or licence may have to meet particular formal requirements in order to be effective; see section 239 of the Australia *Copyright Act 1968* (Cth). Under Australian law, it is not enough to pay for a work to be created in order to also own the copyright

The copyright itself must be expressly transferred in writing. Under the U.S. Copyright Act, a transfer of ownership in copyright must be memorialized in a writing signed by the transferor. For that purpose, ownership in copyright includes exclusive licenses of rights. Thus exclusive licenses, to be effective, must be granted in a written instrument signed by the grantor. No special form of transfer or grant is required. A simple document that identifies the work involved and the rights being granted is sufficient. Non-exclusive grants (often called non-exclusive licenses) need not be in writing under U.S. law. They can be oral or even implied by the behavior of the parties. Transfers of copyright ownership, including exclusive licenses, may and should be recorded in the U.S. Copyright Office. While recording is not required to make the grant effective, it offers important benefits, much like those obtained by recording a deed in a real estate transaction. Copyright may also be licensed. Some jurisdictions may provide that certain classes of copyrighted works be made available under a prescribed statutory license (e.g. musical works in the United States used for radio broadcast or performance). This is also called a compulsory license, because under this scheme, anyone who wishes to copy a covered work does not need the permission of the copyright holder, but instead merely files the proper notice and pays a set fee established by statute (or by an agency decision under statutory guidance) for every copy made. Failure to follow the proper procedures would place the copier at risk of an infringement suit.

Because of the difficulty of following every individual work, copyright collectives or collecting societies and performing rights organizations (such as ASCAP, BMI, and SESAC) have been formed to collect royalties for hundreds (thousands and more) works at once. Though this market solution bypasses the statutory license, the availability of the statutory fee still helps dictate the price per work collective rights organizations charge, driving it down to what avoidance of procedural hassle would justify.

Other Statutes

Copyright law covers the creative or artistic expression of an idea. Patent law covers inventions. Trademark law covers distinctive terms, marks, and names that are used in relation to products or services as indicators of origin, as does (in a similar fashion), Trade dress and Design patents cover the look or appearance of a manufactured or functional article. Trade secret law covers secret or sensitive knowledge or information. Although copyright and trademark laws are theoretically distinct, more than one type of them may cover the same item or subject matter. For example, in the case of the Mickey Mouse cartoon, the image and name of Mickey Mouse would be the subject of trademark legislation, while the cartoon itself would be subject to copyright. Titles and character names from books or movies may also be trademarked while the works from which they are drawn may qualify for copyright.

Another point of distinction is that a copyright (and a patent) is generally subject to a statutorily-determined term, whereas a trademark registration may remain in force indefinitely if the trademark is periodically used and renewal fees continue to be duly paid to the relevant jurisdiction's trade marks office or registry. Once the term of a copyright has expired, the formerly copyrighted work enters the public domain and may be freely used or exploited by anyone. Courts in the United States and the United Kingdom have rejected the doctrine of a common law copyright. Public domain works should not be confused with works that are publicly available. Works posted in the internet for example, are publicly available, but are not generally in the public domain. Copying such works may therefore violate the author's copyright.

There are different approaches to the issue of what is a "copy" of a copyright-protected work. For example, several important rights under United States copyright law exist only for "copies" of works—material objects in which the work is embodied. A three-dimensional counterpart of a two-dimensional drawing is usually not a "copy" of the drawing, under United States copyright law. Thus, the copyright in a drawing of the approach to the Triboro Bridge is not infringed when the bridge approach is built. The copyright law of England is different, a copyright in a drawing is infringed by manufacture of the depicted object. As the House of Lords held in British Leyland Motor Corp. v. Armstrong Patents Co., the manufacture of a tailpipe corresponding to a blueprint of the tailpipe infringes the copyright in the blueprint, and unless a defense applies (as it did in that case) the tailpipe "copyist" is liable for copyright infringement damages.

In the United States, the Copyright Office maintains that typeface designs are not covered by copyright, and it will not accept applications for their registration. In *Tufenkian Import/Export Ventures, Inc. v. Einstein Moomjy, Inc.,* 338 F.3d 127, 132 (2nd Cir. 2003), the United States Court of Appeals for the Second Circuit recognized this rule when it held, "the public domain includes, for example, both the generic shape of the letter 'L' and all of the elaborately more specific 'L's' from the hundreds of years of font designs that have fallen into the public domain." However, if a design is novel and "non-obvious," it may be covered by design patent. Germany (in 1981) passed a special extension to the design patent law (*Geschmacksmustergesetz*) for protecting typeface designs. This permits typefaces being registered as designs in Germany, too. So far, the United States courts have not published any opinions discussing whether a computer program creating a particular font might be intellectual property protected by the copyright laws. England recognized copyright in typeface at least as early as 1916. The current United Kingdom copyright statute, enacted in 1989, expressly refers to copyrights in typeface designs. The British law also applies to designs produced before 1989.

It is legal in several countries including the United Kingdom and the U.S.A to produce alternative versions (for example, in large print or braille) of a copyrighted work to provide improved access to a work for blind and visually impaired persons without receiving prior permission from the copyright holder.

Use of "copyrightable" or "uncopyrightable" as words is rarely helpful from a standpoint of legal analysis and is often misleading or confusing. The problem is that, so long as a writing exists in tangible form, there will usually be *something* to which *some* quantum of copyright protection attaches, even if it is "thin." Thus, a book containing a list of computer-generated code words might be said to be uncopyrightable for lack of originality, a sine-qua-non of copyright protection, or for lack of human authorship. But the work (considered as the whole book) will likely contain an Introduction explaining what the book does, and that portion of the book will almost surely have enough of that minimal degree of creativity that suffices to attract some degree of copyright protection. The proper issue is thus not copyrightability but what kind of copyright protection attaches to which portions of the work.

A professional in the field of library and information science must know various issues pertaining to intellectual property right and copyright because he may come across may such cases of violation of these right.

Treaties and International Agreements

- Berne Convention for the Protection of Literary and Artistic Works of 1886
- Universal Copyright Convention of 1952
- Rome Convention of 1961
- The WTO Agreement on Trade-Related Aspects of Intellectual Property Rights (TRIPS), of 1994
- WIPO Copyright Treaty of 1996
- WIPO Performances and Phonograms Treaty of 1996

REFERENCES

Article I, Section 8, Clause 8 aka Copyright Clause of the United States Constitution

Broussard, Sharee L. (September 2007). *The copyleft movement: creative commons licensing*. Communication Research Trends.

Hull, Geoffrey (2004). *The Recording Industry*. Routledge. pp. 41-42.

Intellectual Property Licensing: Forms and Analysis, by Richard Raysman, Edward A. Pisacreta and Kenneth A. Adler. Law Journal Press.

Levine, David; Michele Boldrin (2008-09-07). *Against intellectual monopoly*. Cambridge University Press.

Mark A. Lemley, "Property, Intellectual Property, and Free Riding" (Abstract); see Table 1: 4-5.

Thomas Jefferson. "Thomas Jefferson to Isaac McPherson". University of Chicago

US v. American Library Association, 539 U.S. 194 (2003).

Weeks, Carly (2008-05-26). "Anti-piracy strategy will help government to spy, critic says". The Globe and Mail.

Appendix

CHILDREN'S INTERNET PROTECTION ACT

The Children's Internet Protection Act (CIPA) is one of a number of bills that the United States Congress has proposed in an attempt to limit children's exposure to pornography and explicit content online. Senator John McCain of Arizona introduced the bill that would become CIPA to the United States Senate in 1999. After various Representatives repeatedly introduced it to the United States House of Representatives, a final version cleared both houses and passed as part of an omnibus spending bill on December 15, 2000. President Bill Clinton signed it into law on December 21, 2000, and it was upheld by the Supreme Court of the United States on June 23, 2003.

Both of Congress's earlier attempts at restricting indecent Internet content, the Communications Decency Act and the Child Online Protection Act, had met with successful Supreme Court challenges on First Amendment grounds. CIPA represented a change in strategy by Congress. While the federal government had no means of directly controlling local school and library boards, many schools and libraries utilized universal service fund discounts, derived from the universal service tax paid by telecommunications users, to purchase Internet access and computers. In passing CIPA, Congress required libraries and schools using these discounts (sometimes called "E-Rate discounts") to purchase and use a "technology protection measure" on every computer connected to the Internet. These conditions were also attached to a small subset of grants authorized through the Library Services and Technology Act (LSTA). CIPA did not provide any additional funds for the purchase of the "technology protection measure."

CIPA requires schools and libraries using E-Rate discounts to operate "a technology protection measure with respect to any of its computers with Internet access that protects against access through such computers to visual depictions that are obscene, child pornography, or harmful to minors..." Such a technology protection measure must be employed "during any use of such computers by minors." The law also provides that the library "may disable the technology protection measure concerned, during use by an adult, to enable access for bona fide research or other lawful purpose." Libraries that do not receive E-Rate discounts do not have any obligation to filter under CIPA.

Suit Challenging CIPA's Constitutionality

On January 17, 2001, the American Library Association voted to challenge CIPA, on the grounds that the law required libraries to unconstitutionally block access to constitutionally protected information on the Internet. It charged first that, because CIPA's enforcement mechanism involved removing federal funds intended to assist disadvantaged facilities, "CIPA runs counter to these federal efforts to close the digital divide for all Americans." Second, it argued that "no filtering software successfully differentiates constitutionally protected speech from illegal speech on the Internet."

Working with the American Civil Liberties Union, the ALA successfully challenged the law in the Court of Appeals for the Eastern District of Pennsylvania. In a 200-page decision, the judges wrote that "in view of the severe limitations of

Index

■■■